CAN GOD IMPROVE MY BALANCE SHEET?

invoking the inner potential

DWARAKNATH REDDY

A Sterling Paperback

STERLING PAPERBACKS
An imprint of
Sterling Publishers (P) Ltd.
A-59, Okhla Industrial Area, Phase-II,
New Delhi-110020.
Tel: 26387070, 26386209; Fax: 91-11-26383788
E-mail: sterlingpublishers@airtelbroadband.in
ghai@nde.vsnl.net.in
www.sterlingpublishers.com

Previously published by the author
Can God Improve My Balance Sheet?
© 2007, Dwaraknath Reddy
ISBN 81 207 3250 2

All rights are reserved.
No part of this publication may be reproduced, stored in a retrieval system or transmitted, in any form or by any means, mechanical, photocopying, recording or otherwise, without prior written permission of the original publisher.

Printed and Published by Sterling Publishers Pvt. Ltd., New Delhi-110 020.

REVIEWS AND OPINIONS

Rare indeed are deep insights from the extremely competitive world of business. To see a successful industrialist believe in the search for truth and in the pre-eminence of natural justice is insightful. The book will add value to those who are committed to action and achievement.

The Hindu

By all counts this is an outstanding work. It harmoniously blends psychology, management, philosophy, religion and spirituality. What it propounds is a beautiful technique of management by integral insight. It can be taken as an exquisite manual on the art of living.

D. P Mandelia
Confidant and advisor to late Sri G.D. Birla

An exhilarating book... written with admirable ability and in a language which is captivating and clear...

A. Rangaswami
Lakshmi General Finance Ltd., Chennai,
Vedic scholar and author

I find the theme of your book to be a magnificent concept.

S. K. Birla
Chairman, Mysore Cements Ltd. Birla Building Kolkatta.

The book is written in a racy style, entertainingly, provocatively.

M.P. Pandit
Scholar and Author, Sri Aurobindo Ashram, Pondicherry.

...inspires lofty thoughts...remarkable and outstanding book which integrates eternal values with business acumen and helps in dealing with operational problems.

S. Radhakrishnan
Professor of Economics
Academy for Promotion of Educational Excellence;
(APEX) Chennai

As one who is connected with HRD in our bank for some time, I found the book to be of relevance to our Senior Executives.

V. Krishnamurthy
Chief Manager, HRD, State Bank of Mysore

OTHER BOOKS BY THE SAME AUTHOR

The Physics of Karma (1992):
(A Requiem to Time)

Birth, Play and Finale of Mind (1998):
(Consciousness Is For Ever)

Sunshine in a Tear-drop:
(Whispers Heard Within)

The Dicey Problem of New Age Science:
(Einstein, Hawking and God at the Casino)

This small token of an immense gratitude
is dedicated to
my father
B.V. Reddy
who has been my inspiration
by being what he was;
he did not have to teach,
he was the teaching.

foreword

The title of the book may appear facetious but it raises an issue very vital and currently relevant. Can spiritual knowledge be strengthening and supportive in pursuing material success?

In this small but remarkable book Shri V Dwaraknath Reddy, a phenomenally successful industrialist and advanced '*sadhak*', answers in the affirmative and outlines a practical spiritual way to material pursuit. He brings a novel approach to a very important area of senior management thinking by showing how to derive strength, peace and happiness in active business life by making the understanding of the laws of life the basic substratum for planning, execution and achievement.

The scriptures, Shri Reddy says, deal with the science of existence. It is the theory of Energy of Life. But for actual benefit we have to apply that knowledge to our personal needs by exploiting that energy.

In logical sequence, Shri Reddy analyses with extraordinary lucidity numerous concepts basic to success in the material realm. Starting with the concept of 'I' that cherishes, desires and faces problems in their fulfilment, he clarifies that you are, at any given time, the resultant point in a lifelong stream of thoughts, feelings and

FOREWORD

responses, and are governed in your further actions by that linear stream. The entire universe around you is similarly shaped by the total effect of interrelated working of the life streams of all the individuals comprised in it. This very perception takes off the strain imposed by the mistaken notion of false power centres and unrealistic possibilities. The relaxation of understanding enables easy and smooth flow of harmonious and joyful action generating maximum efficiency. In the process, false ego and sense of doership are eliminated as you realise that your knowledge and action are limited and are but a fragment of the totality of energy and consciousness. It is the totality that is the causal seed and source, and every effect is a ripple on the total expanse. The insight for progress is derived from the revitalising smile of acceptance symbolising harmony of the individual with the totality.

The utility of meditation is explained as relative stability supporting the whirling wheel of action instead of a passive state distanced from all activity.

The essence of economy is discovered in limited expenditure of the energy of consciousness as outflow of thought just sufficient for the purpose on hand.

A balance sheet is normally understood to be a document prepared by a businessman to represent the financial position at the end of a certain period. Shri Reddy is not confining himself to improving merely the balance sheet of a business but is chalking out the path to improving the balance sheet of *life* itself. The essence of his approach can be said to lie in the most harmonious action with:

(a) a dispassionate and thorough understanding of self and surroundings,

(b) complete faith in the perfection and inviolability of the laws of Nature or Truth,
(c) deep tranquillity and equanimity within, and
(d) genuine goodwill towards all.

This is also the substance of *dharma* and that is why Bhagwan Veda Vyas proclaimed at the end of the Mahabharata:

धर्मादर्थश्च कामश्च स किमर्थ न सेव्यते।।

'From *dharma* flow both *artha* (wealth) and *kama* (pleasure), why is then dharma not pursued?'

Shri Reddy has thus laid out an extremely rational and realistic mode of practising dharma in our mundane lives. Calmness, humility, surrender and such other traits are normally considered by hardheaded executives as weak concepts. But here is an industrialist with proven titanic abilities in practical performance vouchsafing them. His authority should be credible enough. Moreover, the beauty of his exposition is that the perception and understanding generated by the critical analysis of fundamental concepts flood the entire scenario with a new light revealing convincingly the shortest and smoothest path to material success. No strenuous appeals of dos and don'ts to volition are called for.

The author also hints that though the line of thinking that stretches from person to God passes through progressive levels of performance towards perfection, we need not confine our experience of God merely to material achievement but should have the wisdom to realise His other dimension also by abiding in the source of our consciousness. In either case, one has to obey willingly the laws of Nature and that is why the author has analysed meticulously the energy that functions through the mind and as the mind.

The question however remains, 'where is the hand of God in this technique of management?' The great secret is divulged by the author at the end but I would not like to take away the thrill by disclosing it here.

By all counts this is an outstanding work. It harmoniously blends psychology, management, philosophy, religion and spirituality. What it propounds is not only a beautiful technique of management by integral insight but also an excellent mode of *sakam bhakti* which can be easily moulded into *nishkam bhakti* and even *jnan yoga*. It can, therefore, be taken as an exquisite manual in the art of living.

The illustrious work is obviously the product of not only deep study and mature reflection but also earnest practice of its principles by Shri Reddy. I have no doubt that it will prove an invaluable aid to all aspirants of material as well as spiritual success.

New Delhi   Durgaprasad Mandelia

(Shri D P Mandelia was a lifelong confidant and advisor to the late Shri G D Birla)

contents

	foreword	vi
	introduction	1
1	to start with	7
2	the bottom line	9
3	the one who desires	11
4	happiness: to each his own	14
5	the operation of cause	18
6	the options and the choice	22
7	planning for success	27
8	computerised justice	31
9	the power in the pause	37
10	the enemy within	42
11	easy does it	50
12	meditate...who? me?	54
13	doership	61
14	sharing the spoils	65
15	what is your problem?	69
16	the ultimate economy	74
17	at the crossroads	79
18	mind is relativity	84
19	one thing at a time	89
20	afraid of what?	93
21	face all problems equally	95
22	the art of sleeping	98
23	when the mind sleeps	102
24	leadership	108
25	harmony amidst change	112
26	why? because...	116
27	one last word (about lost words)	121
28	epilogue	125

introduction

When you think or talk of advancing towards new heights of achievement and success that you have not scaled as yet, your plan of action cannot be that somehow you will conspire to make luck strike you and lightning strike your adversaries. Though commendably simple and straightforward, both those objects seem to be beyond your powers of management or manipulation.

The success you aspire to must be won by invoking the inner potential in yourself. You must become the best you can be. You cannot be more than your full potential, but why should you be less? Your ambition and urge confirm the faith you have in yourself. You are not denying that untapped potential could be abiding in you, but the proof has to lie in its manifesting itself in performance. The inherent capability must be brought out and materialised. That is what is meant by invocation. And that has to be done by you, by working upon yourself diligently. No outsider can be accommodated in this implementation, which is a transaction between you as you are today, and you as you can be in future.

You have accepted certain premises as unquestionable and unavoidable, and those have defined your tools and skills and strengths for your work. Persisting with them has given you whatever you have gained or achieved so far and may, by blunt impact and brute force, take you a little farther too. But if you would hold your hand for a while and calmly reassess the worth and validity of those for conclusions, you would arrive at startling discoveries of the laws of processes, the environment in which people interact, the mechanics of integrated action and the dispensation of results. Such understanding would keep you in harmony with the energy system that life is, reinforcing strengths and eliminating conflicts, thereby releasing the power (be it repeated) that you possess even now but are unable to utilise to your advantage.

This new sense and sensibility dawned on me at midday (if you will pardon the mix-up)! I had equipped myself with a Master of Science degree in chemical engineering from USA and joined my father in starting and developing a family-owned business in a food-processing industry. The untimely death of an elder brother at the age of thirty-seven, and the demise of my father not long thereafter, left me suddenly alone carrying an unequal burden. Obviously, I needed all the strengths I could muster, but how does one go about it? You may do more of what you did before, and maybe do it a little better too, but to break out into a new dimension altogether, you reach out for...what? how?... when you do not know what or how.

Fortunately for me, I did not look then for *performance*; instead, I looked for *personal integration*. Demand brings the supply. I listened and I contemplated without compromising on my output of diligent work. Give me credit for just one thing; I was earnest. And the rest happened—it has to, for such is the law of nature.

It was soon evident to me that all the new rays of lights that I was now becoming aware of, would focus into one spot of effulgence, which would be the real potential of my seeking mind. This conviction was all the strength and capability I needed. In harmony with it, I lived and worked.

A lot of success came my way. Be it said that if it had not come, it would have changed nothing. The unchanging law of gravity must be seen alike in the falling rock and the floating feather. A law does not ever yield its rightful rigidity. If it did, it would be no law. What I had perceived was the universal law of mental processes and material consequences. All results were according to that consistent law. My satisfaction or sadness arising from results in a personal sense could not be the criterion for the validity of the law.

Anyhow success came. Friends might have felt inclined to mock the 'monk' whose disinclination towards accepted indulgences could be forgiven (and hopefully corrected later by them), but whose sustained interest in a search for some reality beyond one's known and commonly experienced identity was totally unworthy and inexcusable. But when the small factory, sustained by its steady growth, could become the national leader in the industry, one had to concede grudgingly that there was 'something' in its leader's approach to life and work. One common conclusion is to say it is 'luck'. Many said that. I have no quarrel with this.

In any field there is the *PURE* science and there is the *APPLIED* science. Scriptures deal with the Science of Total Existence. It is the theory of the Energy of Life. To make that knowledge useful to our personal needs, scriptures of the world do give us practical applications and systems, and circuit diagrams. Leave volts and amps and ohms and watts to the scientist, but don't let your aversion for those words prevent you from using electricity for comfort and entertainment in your home. So, ignore 'God' if you prefer to do so, but use, even exploit, the energy of life. Only remember, to use an energy safely one should know enough not to do the wrong things. You need not know volts and watts but you should know that you do not stick your fingers into an exposed socket.

All that time we spend in factory, field and office is the necessary price we pay for providing the means through which each one of us finds happiness in oneself in accordance with one's preferences. That happiness often has its centre in the family, for it is there that associations, demands, desires, sacrifices and expectations are the strongest. It is the same person that acts all day in the outside environment that goes home in the evening—and his mind goes with him.

Basically transaction between persons continues with wife, parents, children, visiting relatives and domestic helpers replacing (not in that order please!) board of directors, managers, competitors, customers, government and labour. And the same rules of understanding and interacting hold good.

Therefore, one who has learned the laws of consciousness and their rightful application to mental management, performs with equal felicity at home, contributing joy, peace and love to the charmed circle.

Whoever deals with another—and, who doesn't?—is then a manager, managing that situation. You do not need to be the Chief Executive or Managing Director of a company to be concerned about the balance sheet. It is of paramount concern to all of us in all walks of life, because in a wider sense, it stands for the essence of living. But sadly, it does not ring true except when the focus is on making a million. As though a happy home is not itself worth a million, and millions are worth anything without happiness at home!

INTRODUCTION

In my hours of crises, and the days of trial and test that followed, I did not surrender to cynicism or despair or bravado. My concern was not to determine then and there whether there was, or had ever been, a God (or gods), whether there was justice in events or sense in life, whether morality and success are compatible. If someone had given me specific and succinct answers to such questions, by what parameters could I have evaluated their validity? In real terms, what could be my gain? Ultimately, one has to discover the answers for oneself.

I stayed with what I believed to be a greater and more fundamental wisdom on the subject. I had read the words of a Master. 'Instead of searching for the proof of truth which you do not know, go through the proofs you have of what you believe you know.' I recognised therein the direction in which I should proceed to invoke my inner potential. It worked.

I was smiling to myself as I mused: how I wish I could share this with my friends (never mind if it is leaked out to my competitors), and move them out of the habituated groove of an insufficient methodology.

Wiser men than me are offering us deep insights in scriptural terms, but we remain untouched. If they tell us, 'Study the Bhagawad Gita, it is a handbook for daily living', we cannot get motivated. I was like that myself. But now if, with conviction, I can tell my friends, *'You want to know how to make a million through the BHAGAWAD GITA?'* will not their ears stand up? And I know they will grasp the points of the narration. They (like me) can smell money. Then they (like me) will make that million.

Just at that moment you trooped in, nose a little upturned on seeing me, and said with a sneer: *'Ah, go on.*

You and your blind belief. Tell me one thing: CAN YOUR GOD IMPROVE MY BALANCE SHEET?'

1

to start with

'Can YOUR God improve my balance sheet?' were your exact words. There was even more to the tone than the bare meaning of the words. The cynicism, and the hardly veiled resentment that sought to banish any discussion by the wording of the question itself, were not missed, but let that be between you and me. I have preferred to soften the caption into *'Can God improve my balance sheet?,'* deleting the attempted provocation.

Let me ask you now: what is the content of that word *'GOD'* in your present usage and understanding? You tell me.

You may say: *'The word is sound without substance. Hasn't a wise realist said that if there were no God, man would need to invent one? That had to happen. So your God—okay, God—is a palliative, the answer to questions that cannot be answered, the light that is claimed to exist but will never be seen. He is the Great Escape.'*

Or, you may say: *'God is the creator of the universe. He made the earth and put life upon it. He supports and rewards the virtuous and He punishes the sinner—that kind of thing.'*

You are not too sure, so you seem uncomfortable. 'So...?' I prod you on.

'*Well, that is it. The rest is up to us. We have to live our lives the way we want and can. I want success. I want profits. I work for it. I plan, I strive. Why bring God into it? You mean He has the time or the interest to get involved in my business? Would you have me keep a vacant chair in the board room for the unheralded visit?*'

Good sarcasm, but I have not been reduced to a heap of ashes. May I talk?

2
the bottom line

What is the effective bottom line of your balance sheet? Hopefully, the profit you have made, is it not?

Why is it so important? Is it an end in itself? Not exactly, but it is the means to all that you desire and have striven for.

Meaning? Meaning just that, for with the profits, you can grow, expand your business, buy more machines, produce and sell more, and earn larger profits over again. You can spend more on yourself and live the way you have always wanted to live. You may even be able to help others whose welfare is dear to you.

Quite so. Even though you earned a huge profit, if you could not translate it into the satisfaction of your desires, it would have meant nothing. It is the happiness that comes from the fulfilment of desires that is sought and striven for.

So really the bottom line is *HAPPINESS*. Happiness or its absence, or its opposite, is not an output or attribute of the mechanical corporate structure, for its locus can only be in *you*, the person. And so, an improvement of the balance sheet is, in real terms, the scenario that ensures *your* greater happiness.

Beneath and beyond the unthinking usage of habituated language, there is only one balance sheet that man is concerned about, and that is his personal *inner* balance sheet that balances sorrow and delight. You were wiser than you realised when you said 'my balance sheet' even while you meant 'my company's balance sheet'.

You may say: *'There is no great significance to what you have said. Once the profits come, I do the things that make me happy.'* Agreed, and we will proceed on that basis, but be it admitted that money or material success, and happiness, are not synonyms—one does not inevitably flow from the other.

There are problems of poverty, and there are problems of prosperity; and often enough the latter are more treacherous than the former.

Contentment may not survive in a golden cage.

But of course, that is not our pressing problem at this moment. We are in the mood to say, 'Never mind. Find me a golden cage.'

So be it.

3

the one who desires

'*If wishes were horses...*' the old proverb needs to be amended. If wishes were horses, there would be no derby, for everyone would ride his horse to victory. In real life we have our wishes to fulfil, on which depends our happiness, but as likely as not—indeed more likely than not—success eludes us. It is then we say, 'There is a problem.' When things go the way that suits us, when action has produced the results we desired, all is well with the world; but when our expectations are belied and the outstretched hand has been denied the fruit it longed to hold, we call that a problem. Obviously, something is a problem when it has gone wrong. How can it be a problem if it is just the way it should be, if it is right the way it is? So when we determine that it is a problem, meaning it should not be thus, we have our own idea of how rightness should be, meaning how it should have been instead of the way it actually turned out to be. We have decided what is right (suits us) and what is wrong (does not suit us) in the given situation.

If you could have willed your wishes into fruition and satisfied your desires of the day, no doubt your gain would have been the loss of someone else—who otherwise exults when you sulk—and the *problem* would be his instead. So, with limited supply and unlimited demand, problems remain, while only the focus of personal interest shifts. If supply increases, demand increases too and even faster, so that is no answer.

What then are we mouthing platitudes for, of peace and plenty and manna?

'*I don't,*' you say, '*this is a dog-eat-dog world*. We are talking of my balance sheet, remember?'

I will go along with you on that. How to be the eating dog and not become the eaten dog, that is the question. (Hamlet said it a little differently.)

But you must go along with me with some patience and trust. No two situations are alike and no two men are alike. Through this bewildering maze of variety, if we aspire for consistency of achievement, we must take the time and the trouble to find out the mechanics of happiness and the workings of human minds. To do this purposefully and intently there is only one area available to scrutiny and that is ONESELF. No matter that it is the only area, for it is a *sufficient* area. Having completed one's study therein, it will be seen that no related question remains unanswered and all the data required to formulate a perfect plan of action are in hand.

But you must sit down for the task. We are willing to spend the prime of our life learning to start work as a doctor or an engineer, or to acquire skills in any externalised activity, but it seldom occurs to one to set aside a little time and energy to look at the structuring of our own mental processes. This is just like you have looked at ten thousand objects since morning today, and given them the attention of sight perception, but have not for once given a thought to the eye that perceived them.

THE ONE WHO DESIRES

'I got you', you say with diabolical glee, *'what need is there for me to think of the eye? If I kept doing so, I will, more likely, trip and fall down.'* You are right and wrong. The example is to force you into fresh thinking. You need not know the eye that sees, to deal with what is seen, but the 'I' that is you, this 'I' that makes use of the eye and of all perceptions and knowledge, that exudes desire and longs for the fruit, that seeks happiness and despairs in failure, this 'I' that says there is a problem—have you ever paid attention to this 'I'?

Each one of us is an 'I'. It is this 'I' that identifies you, him, them, it, and all the world of still objects and moving events. It is 'I' that is the centre of the mind, initiating action and receiving the result. Here is the source and sensing of all that exists.

This 'I' is true, whatever else be false. This 'I' is imminent whatever else is distant. This 'I' is immediate, whatever else is lost in the mists of time. How shall I sally forth into a brave world for conquest, not knowing the working of 'I' that is me?

4

happiness: to each his own

The 'person' that you are at this moment, how did it come to pass that you are precisely what you are and not something else? We are talking about you, the person, the personality, the sum total of the mind that expresses through you and as you, a specific construct of identification, memory, predilections, desires, fears, hopes, joys and sorrows—all this together at once, for that is what you are. Are you not THAT in the *continuity* of your life? Leave aside speculation, the unknown, the unknowable or the beliefs of others. Of what use are they to you? You have within the focus of your gaze the experienced reality of yourself that cannot be gainsaid, and you need nothing besides.

What is happiness to you today? Surely it is not the catalogued content of history or tradition, but something that your mind decrees, prescribes, pursues and persuades. There is nothing universal or sacrosanct about it. How has your mind arrived at its choice? At the prompting of memory—how else?

All one's life one seeks happiness, and you have done the same. From infancy there have been stimuli or experiences. Several have been pleasurable and others have offended you through pain or distaste. All of them have left an impression upon the faculty called memory. You and your memory are never apart. To serve your incessant quest for happiness, memory formulates that aspect of your recorded appreciation which becomes relevant to the present instant, and shapes it into your desire. The mind says, 'If I can do this now, if I can obtain this result, I will be happy.'

Why should there be a desire at all, leading to action of uncertain benefit? Why don't I stay free of desire altogether?

Because I cannot! Two facts emerge as invariable truths about the mind—your mind or mine or of anyone else of all times. First, the compulsive urge to be happy is the very nature of life. It is not cultivated, or gained as knowledge imparted to one. It is the inherent intrinsic urge of all that live.

Second, there is an equally inherent intrinsic conviction that abiding happiness can be secured and protected through a process of acquisition and relationships; that this world of men and raw materials can give us complete contentment. That is why we follow the quest for a life time, never despairing that the method of our pursuit may be wrong. This impulsive quest can be formulated in two ways, both really amounting to the same sense: become happy through gaining the pleasant, or become happy through avoiding the unpleasant. One is simple and positive, the other is a double negative which denotes the same end.

Obviously, there can be no demand for securing happiness from one who is always abiding in unbroken happiness. The fact that desires spring unabated in the human psyche is proof of a sense of incompleteness or inadequacy in every human being, no matter how one is placed in life, how much he is blessed with possessions, how he is rewarded for the effort. It means that action and result in some way fail again and again to satisfy the instinct for unbroken happiness in man. Nor, as already observed, can man quit the game any more than he can abandon the feeling of hunger peeved at its endless recurrence and all the tiresome toil in coping up with the interminable demands of the stomach. For, what is natural to birth cannot be denied by an exercise of will.

So, in our case we shall seek fulfilment—let it be business as usual!—but with the added understanding that a 'person' is unique, being the end-product at this instant of all the life he has lived so far, the events and impulses that made him happy or sad and were registered as such in his own and very personal memory. He is now the last point of a line that represents his felt life so far, a point that has been arrived at because he was, moment after moment, and event after event, in his life the particular responding and recording entity that he was.

In other words, there is no uncertainty in all this, no indeterminable or extraneous factor, and most specifically nothing of what one loosely terms as luck or chance. There is only the inevitability of consistent law and reason. You are now and here the quintessence of a lifetime, the entity shaped by the thoughts and feelings and responses from your birth till today, the final point so far to which your entire past has prepared and propelled you. But you are not a point set adrift; you are held by a linear link that imparts direction and momentum to your next movement.

Happiness to you is an equation framed by this truth of your being in this instant. It is what your mind, on its own terms, derived with reference to its own memories, construes as pleasant, and therefore, worthy of repetition.

Consequently, you wish to launch such action as can find expression in the environment available to you, to interact with other forces as necessary, and create the desired fruit of all this labour.

But there are other forces to contend with. How are they structured? What are the limitations and possibilities of your success?

the operation of cause

Any change has to be 'caused'. Any movement can be brought about only by application of energy. Energy is not perceivable as such, but is inferred from the effect it causes. Electricity is not seen, but it causes light in the bulb, motion in the fan, and sound in the radio.

Two simple rules emerge: *a)* without cause, there can be no effect; *b)* as the cause, so the effect. This means cause is transformed into effect and what is inherently potential in the cause can alone be the nature of the manifested effect. Fire will burn and water will wet. It will be that way; it cannot be another way.

The mind is the expression of life-energy. The mind is ever in movement, conceiving thoughts, shaping desires, assembling plans, and initiating follow-up physical action in oneself and in others. This *energy* which manifests as mental activity which is the precursor to physical activity is, in its potential state, the *causal body* that manifests the cognised *thought* which is the 'subtle body' of mentation, and this in turn, leads to physical and perceivable *action* through the 'gross body' of flesh and bone.

Memory resides in and operates through the causal aspect of consciousness. Memory is what gives continuity to one's life, and is therefore, the sustainer of a persisting identity. It is constituted of all that have been *cognised* as events and impressions. All these are stored in the vaults of memory, which return to facilitate future *re-cognition*.

The contents of one's memory are not seen as such, for that is the totality of unmanifested cause, and we know that cause is not perceivable in the causal frame, but can be perceived only when it manifests. The manifestation of consciousness is THOUGHT, the unit of mental mechanics, the building block of the phenomenal universe. We may say consciousness gives rise to thought, as electricity gives rise to light.

AS YOU THINK, SO YOU ACT. The validity of the statement is self-evident. But you do not enjoy unlimited freedom in hosting your thoughts. You are already a defined and demarcated entity in terms of your stored memory, which is the 'causal' source of what will be claimed by you in the secondary stage of 'subtle' expression as 'my thought' or 'my knowledge'. The prior conditioning of the moment to follow is the operational process of mentation.

In fact, you exist in your thought through your thoughts, and as your thoughts. To have a thought is, in other words, to know the content of the thought. A thought, any thought, is constructed as a subject–object relationship. 'I know this' is the form of any thought. 'I' is the knower, the *subject,* the constant capability of knowing. 'Know' is the process of knowing, the functioning of the capability. 'This' is the *object* that is known, the variable from thought to thought. Light being the same, the objects revealed by the light can be many.

The entity 'I' is alive in being conscious, and to be conscious is to be aware of thoughts. To be without thoughts would mean being without response to external stimuli, to be incapable of manifesting a subject– object relationship. Without that, there is nothing to validate the continuing identity of the conscious entity, and that is precisely what our deep sleep state is.

That is the sense of the famous dictum of Descartes: *Cogito Ergo Sum* (I think, therefore I am).

It follows that you, the person, have the existence that you attribute to yourself only in the subtle and gross levels, where thought is created and activated, and so you cannot manipulate the action at the source, that is in the causal state.

No doubt it is the causal state of your own life-energy and it is inextricably linked up with you through holding the momentum of your memory. But each passing moment brings you out as the *product* of that energy and not as its master.

At any given moment, your causal state is a congealed mass of your entire past. Does this obviously imply that only what is contained therein can manifest out of it? This may sound as inflexible determinism, but we shall see that it is a limitation rather than a fixed rigidity. Our purpose so far has been to see the limits of possibility, thus to become enabled to utilise our energies purposefully, which otherwise tend to get frittered away in futile protests or untenable ambitions. Having seen that *'as we think, so we act'*, we proceed to recognise that *'as we act, so we become'*. And thus the way we act in the present, prompted and instructed by the past, will shape our immediate future. And this future, when experienced, will carry its impression back into memory, altering to that extent the content and texture of the causal energy that will return another day. This is the continuing story of life.

6

the options and the choice

Take the case of a man with a strong urge to gamble. Do you know of any casino owner who gambled away his den? Not likely, for he knows precisely how the odds are loaded in the operation of this *'game of skill'*, and he prospers. But one friend is well (or ill?) on the way to disaster.

Come evening, and his mind says, *'Let me hasten to the casino—today I will make a kill.'* At once the same mind also says, *'You could lose again. Like yesterday and the day before. You cannot afford any more losses.'*

There are no two minds in him, as there aren't in you or in me. But the mind is not a static thing, it is structured for movement and change, it must release energy. Energy flows when there is 'potential difference', as water or air flows from high pressure to low pressure, as electric current flows from positive to negative. Thus the movement confirms that there have to be two levels of perception in the mind, that is within oneself, and therefore, in a manner of speaking, two voices can be heard, opening up the possibility of deviating from, or continuing upon, the line that represents the past leading to this point in time and mood.

THE OPTIONS AND THE CHOICE

We may call these the voice of the 'lower self' when it resists change into what is perceived as better, and as the 'higher self' when it prompts such a change. But it is just helpful terminology for easy comprehension, even as one may refer to a person's lower body and higher body, meaning the legs or the trunk. One man is one self (being oneself) and has one mind. The return of the prodigal is the theme in life, the secret urge that recalls the wanderer to his home, and brings the mind back to rest in its source. 'What is that source?' Never mind, it does not concern us when we are hell-bent on wandering. So without confusion let us continue our analysis through the discussion of the twin voices.

The lower self is reluctant to make the personal effort and 'sacrifice' the self-gratification that change demands. To the lazy and indulgent, it is easier to maintain status quo, to stay on the line of yesterday nudged by its momentum. To be honest, in accepting the higher when it is visible, calls for heroism—but habit makes cowards of us.

So the easy mind says, *'Yesterday was just bad luck. You will see today.'* And feeling uncomfortable at its inability to sound convincing, adds, *'I need some fun, don't I? I work and earn. I need relaxation too.'*

The chastising mind says, 'You know you are playing a mug's game. If you win in one throw, you will lose that and much more too soon thereafter. You have a wife and two kids. It is not that you have no love for them. But this love of self-indulgence has become your dominant desire. Look at the misery you are causing to those that trusted you and deserve a better deal!'

'I don't deny all that', says the lower self, for how can the inherent immediate knowledge within oneself be denied? It may not be heeded, but it has to be heard.

Thus two forces are being applied at one point simultaneously. What will be the result? It is simple physics that it can be determined through the parallelogram of forces.

Consider a ball at point O. The ball is hit at one and the same time by two sticks. One stick hits it in direction OA with a force equal to four units. This is depicted as a line OA that is four units in length. The other stick hits the ball in the direction OB with a force of three units. So this is depicted by line OB three units in length.

Now, obviously the ball will not go exactly in direction OA or direction OB, for its response must express the impact of both the forces in one movement. To find out precisely which way the ball will travel and where it will stop, the parallelogram of which OA and OB are the sides is completed. The diagonal OC is the vector of the two forces. Its direction is resolved, as also its magnitude, which calculation or measurement will show precisely.

If OA (4 units) and OB (3 units) are at right angles to each other, OC will be the square root of the sum of $OA^2 + OB^2$.

$$\sqrt{4^2 + 3^2} \ = \ \sqrt{16 + 9} \ = \ \sqrt{25} \ = \ 5$$

Therefore, in this case the ball will travel five units along the diagonal and stop there.

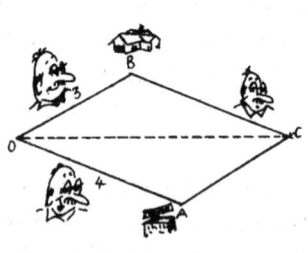

Figure: 6.1

Replace the ball with our friend, and the sticks with the two inner voices that are pulling him or pushing him in two directions and measure the intensity of each impulse (the do-it and the don't-do-it). Draw the lines mentally-casino-bound and mentally-home-bound. And conceding that today his old love could not be abandoned altogether you have recorded the conflict and the limited conquest along the diagonal (see Figure 6.1).

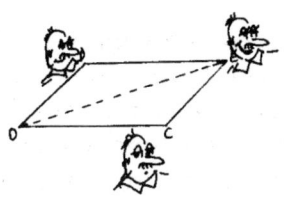

Figure: 6.2

This means that our friend ended up at the casino (rather shame-faced) and gambled (less damaging) and left repentant (though not totally broke). He is not cured but he is slightly changed. Tomorrow his natural state will be depicted by OC of less damaging strength which is itself a happy departure from OA, and if the benevolent voice of the higher self has not despaired (it has not, and will not so easily) the redeeming impact will be OD, hopefully with greater vigour. Thus tomorrow's parallelogram will groove the personality into OE (see Figure 6.2).

The progress may be maintained, or it may be lost and we may lose our man in the tunnels of mental despair or reaction. Who can predict the hidden contents of the causal consciousness, blended of a myriad of lifetime experiences, shuffled and stacked up, not in the chronological order of occurrence but on an intricate, complex, computerised determination of perception, pleasure, desire and need of a changing wayward person? What is the significance of your words 'remembered' and 'forgotten' any more when the cause exists and is the only reality though then remaining unknown (is that 'forgetfulness'?) and your thought is born out of that causal 'forgetfulness' and placed before your cognition (you call that 'remembrance'?) So leave aside the superficial and unrewarding distinctions of subconscious or unconscious, and come to grips with the cause and the effect, the unmanifest and the manifest.

Within this scheme we are left with a marginal play of choice and self-determination, but in the overall context, we see that we are at any given moment what we have made of ourselves. We can neither blame it on others, nor can we wish it away.

The truth of the present moment is a mighty reality shaped on the anvil of Time by the total movement of phenomena. We are all parts of it. As cause produces effect, which in turn becomes the cause for the subsequent effect, there is a chronological continuity in the material flux and a memory-structured continuity in consciousness. We can neither escape the movement nor can we command it. *But we need not suffer in it.* If we suffer it is only because we have not cared to understand the law of the energy by which we exist and can prosper, and in our ignorance are falling foul of it. It is needless. To know the law is to be able to harmonise with it, and that harmony is the happiness we so desperately seek.

7

planning for success

You have become aware of a desire in yourself. This desire we are looking at now is but one more in an endless succession and will not be the last, for to desire and to seek is the thrust of life. There is this nameless timeless urge for abiding happiness which has haunted all humans all their lives. The demand for a certain object now seems a matter of your choice but the demand for happiness is a choiceless obsession bestowed by birth itself.

That you plan to achieve the goal or object of your desire is natural. It may be small or mighty. It may be a cup of coffee, or clinching a large business deal, or becoming the prime minister of the country. There are related memories in you that spell out to you the reward of that attainment, and it is that pleasure that is anticipated. Therein is your motivation for action. We love to serve ourselves, for we love ourselves. You love the wife because you love that loving of the wife, and the experiencing centre of that love is in yourself. That again is the name of life. This is no cynicism or condemnation, it is but honest recognition of what is and how it has always been.

Let us proceed now to clinch the business. A big deal is coming up and it can keep your plant humming for months ... and it can repeat itself ... and it could lead to similar orders from two others ... the profit margin can be (hush, surveillance is the word to watch today!) ... and with that money you can order more machinery.

Easy now, if you don't mind. Quieten the mind. Conserve mental energy and use it just as much as is essential—you cannot have too much of it.

Our 'Operation Big-Deal' involves several factors and persons. You are but one of them, an important one no doubt, but do not forget you are one amongst many. What exactly is the order of importance? Your multi-million-rupee Mercedes car cannot budge an inch on the journey when you are all set to go, if there is no air in the tyres, and the air doesn't cost a nickel! How do you draw up the list?

There is the customer with his calculations and priorities that need not accommodate yours all the way. There are the competitors clawing for the same loaves and waiting to outwit you. There are your teammates who must play their assigned or intuited parts as the action proceeds. There are governmental policies and rules that can change suddenly and wreck all the calculations. There may even be a war in a distant land whose widening ripples can rock your boat violently.

True and fair enough, we draw the lines, trust the validity of our studied assessments, and launch the action, but it needs to be conceded that the result depends upon the play and interplay of many factors of which real control in your hands seems to be only with regard to one of them—namely, yourself. And even there, how predictable are you to yourself?

The day of decision is approaching. All the intelligence available to you has been utilised to process the inquiry;

samples and specifications have been meticulously submitted; and there is little else that can be done before the hour strikes.

Wipe the sweat off your brow. There was work to be done and you have done it well. Right now is the period of lull, and can you not wait it out quietly? There is no scope for useful work right now, but you are more restless, more 'active' in unproductive thought, than when you were working on the project. Your mind is conjuring up various scenarios, suppose this ... suppose that ... suppose the fellow has ... suppose by oversight ... Is there an end to suppositions? What happens is just that *one* thing that does happen, but before the happening, imagination can conceive of numberless possibilities. Truth is one, falsehood has endless variety. If I ask you 'what is your name?' the answer is just one, but if I ask you 'what is not your name?' and if you start on an answer to that, where and when will you stop? Can you exhaust the list of names that are not your name?

Kindergarten stuff, you mock me. I don't mind. But tell me why you exhaust yourself with endless variations of what the future might unfold, fearing each adverse probability that may not materialise, and even if it does, should be faced without fear and confusion, but must be met with stoic acceptance and adequate response. For, it is *then* that you must be in full command of yourself, be alert to the changed circumstances, and compute with speed and precision if there be any chance left to recover. Suppose there is a leeway for negotiation, suppose some significant advantage that your offer envisages has not been adequately appreciated in the buyer's evaluation of competitors' offers, you have to move in with composure, dignity and firm resolve. Energy is needed for it, also freshness and relaxation. But if you are panting already from the fruitless exertions of a frenzied imagination, you have defeated yourself much before the finishing line.

All right, I will give you the benefit of doubt. You have been in cool command. You have done everything right and solid. You cannot be faulted. That you have a desire—no fault there. That you plan for its fulfilment and act diligently—fine. That naturally you are expectant and await the enjoyment of the fruits of your labour—what can be wrong in that?

There ... the hour strikes. You have lost the order. You did everything you could even after the first announcement, but finally the curtain has been rung down. You have lost.

Now is the time for a slow-motion study, the frame-by-frame observation of the anatomy of 'failure'; of you facing the moment of 'defeat'.

8

computerised justice

You do not plant a thousand mango trees and hope that one of them may produce apples! You do not expect that somewhere somehow water will run up a gradient. Or that fire will freeze or that a rock will melt. Nature remains natural. All things abide eternally in their intrinsic *nature,* with never a deviation, for cause must produce its result, true to itself—there is no other way. Nature knows this, and Nature does not grumble; Nature has no problem, for everything is for ever right. The law of causation, that is the continuing flow of cause to effect, is inviolable; it is also exquisite in its grandeur and faultless in its justice.

Yet man, who ought to be the highest evolved manifestation of Nature, is convinced that the 'unnatural' is a possibility and often a fact of his experience. He asserts that 'accidents' happen and 'ill-luck' alters a result. Nature must be amused to observe that a concept of the unnatural in the self-esteemed human must be the only unnatural aspect in creation! For in thinking so, man is asserting that a choice of results is available at a given point in the action. But, given the fixity of the cause at the moment, how can there be anything else but the one effect that expresses the truth and reality of that cause? Cause, while yet to manifest, is unknown and invisible, and reveals itself only when we perceive it transformed into manifested effect. At that stage one can infer and speculate on what the cause might have been, but to believe that there is a choice of effects in the straight-line extension of the cause–effect continuum is sadly an insult to intelligence.

Then again, since every cause had its precedent cause, causation as it has related to you, moulded you, and been expressed through your experience of life, cannot be a closed circle with its beginning and end within you. It must necessarily be part of a total movement in which you are one 'I' centre of perception and reaction. Then, there must similarly be as many such centres as you recognise as 'him', 'her' and 'them'. To be individual movements within one total current would obviously be like localised eddies of whirling water within the total flow of a river. Such eddies seem to have a self-generated energy and movement, but in truth, they are only caused by the current of the flooded river and are inevitable natural effects in the dynamics of the surging movement.

The unerring virtuosity of the law of causation (no cause, no effect; as the cause, so the effect) has to be sustained in relation to every centre where it is felt, that is to say, for every individual involved in the total action. Each one can demand 'was justice done to me?', and if it was not, one can no longer talk of a law of nature, for laws of nature cannot, just cannot, err.

So, every happening *MUST HAVE* a rightness to it. Who can clearly discern and experience spontaneously that rightness in every occurrence? Only he that knows the validity of the law, and has a view of the total area of its operation so that he can monitor its functioning, can say so. Who is that one? Where is he seated? Never mind. We can't jump the gun. Know for *now* that it is *not you* that has to wait till the eddy merges its mistaken separate identity in the unitary identity of the river. You are now only one eddy in the current. But should that prevent you from appreciating the relative aspects of the eddy and the river?

To return to our big deal, quite a few 'I' centres (individuals) were involved in it. Many lines of cause–effect continuity converged upon this action. Each one of them, in the unbroken succession of life, had arrived upon this stage in the drama to play a part and partake of the total effect at this moment. And it was incumbent upon the law to see that the result offered justice and nothing but justice to *each* participant in personal terms.

Such distribution of the fruits of action would be unassailable, for who could fault the upholding of justice without favour or prejudice? If that is not the meaning and method of universal love, tell me, what is?

To state it a little differently, there is a *deserving* at every moment in the continuing unfolding of one's personal life, an experience *deserved* by the individual on his own responsibility and willed conduct up to that instant, and the wondrous law of causation ensures that exactly what is deserved is meted out. Let it be repeated *ad nauseum* that there is not an alien on a remote perch that is imposing despotic decrees upon hapless victims. We are talking of a law serenely in command, than which any arrangement more equal, more just, more beautiful, more loving, cannot be conceived.

When you talk of 'luck' you are not talking of how 'deserving', are you? For what can be luck in getting what you deserve? The packet on pay-day is not the man's luck! But the winning of a lottery, isn't that luck? No, that too is only the confirmation of the mathematical assertion of the law of probability. 'But it happened to my wicked neighbour who is already loaded' you bemoan (meaning you know who deserved it better). 'The lucky...'

I sympathise with you, my friend, but a law accepts no exceptions. His getting it was deserved, as truly as your missing it by one door number was also deserved.

It has already been pointed out that the effects you perceive are not a chronological series of manifesting causes that you identify from your personal knowledge or diary and allot a sequence. Your knowledge is limited and is but a fragment in the totality of consciousness. It is the totality that is the causal seed and source, and every effect is a ripple upon the total expanse. You can understand the law even from your personal centre, but that does not transpose you into the true centre of the total energy. Your data remains limited. That is why you are inclined to dispute and disapprove the reward which a higher authority has sanctioned to your neighbour. Jealousy can be indulged in by you and me (and hope it will be forgiven) but the law knows no jealousy, no prejudice, no favour. Justice is bound by its own laws, and does not seek to hurt or please.

In the computerised record of all thoughts and deeds within consciousness—the keying-in is evidently a perfect, infallible, self-contained procedure by virtue of every thought and deed being a movement in consciousness itself, and not external to it—there is the programming according to causal law which rightly determines which effect time has ripened for manifestation in the present moment. Naturally, you could not be acquainted with your neighbour's causal balance, since you cannot know even your own. But let us be gracious enough to concede that somewhere down the line of his existence, he has earned the right to pip you to the post on the lottery.

'What perversity is this conclusion?' No, my friend, no perversity. Recapture the law of operation of life with objective honesty. Upon the voyage that is undertaken in quest of personal fulfilment, causation governs the movement of your mind as totally as gravity governs the movement of your body, and they are both eternal and inviolable laws.

You have not been seeing this because you are obsessed with desire. You have linked the longed for happiness with a certain result, and made it a *demand.* You must have it your way.

But by what moral or temporal sovereignty can you insist upon having it your way? Look at all the movements of individual energies that converged upon this focus of action and contributed towards shaping the result? What *had* to be was shaped by the *total movement,* but what you say it *should* be is being pronounced by your *individual movement.* The *fact* of the result expresses the law's rightness, and therefore, the 'deserving'. The *wish* for a certain result expresses the individual's perversity and therefore the 'desiring'.

In terms of yourself you had a choice in action at each moment as the two voices of your evolving personality spoke either in support of status quo, or in support of change. Your decisions were made along the vector of the two forces. *Thereafter,* no claims can be made upon the *past* moment, be it a lost chance or a grasped opportunity. The result has to flow choicelessly, representing your resolved truth. THIS is the meaning of surmising that what HAS to be, that alone WILL be. To say so is not an exertion in futility, not an expression of failure. To see the workings of a law rightly is not the weakness of a despairing mind, or of an enslaved citizen, but the strength of a courageous one that can live with the truth. The word 'fate' is loosely bandied, but who cares to know its meaning?

So, there is a *deserving* and a *desiring*. When it happens, as it not infrequently does, that what you desire (knowingly) is also what you deserve (unknowingly), good for you and there is no stopping you then. 'I did it ... I told you so ... There was no way it could be otherwise ... I tell you, you can make things happen ...' We have nothing against the celebration. It is right and natural that we relate action and result, that we desire and anticipate, that we enjoy holding and eating the sweet fruit when it has landed in our hands.

But instead if you had to taste the bitterness of failure, what then? You were not waiting in controlled anticipation to see which number would get picked up, you had decided that it has to be your number. You could not be bothered about what you deserved, you said it has to be what you demanded, what you had predetermined under the dictates of your personal desire.

But you are not the lawmaker! You cannot be the river when you are the eddy. You can be, but a lot of understanding has to precede the transcendence. Right now we are looking at personal profit rooted where we are, and are not talking of any transcendence.

And, you are angry. Angry about the things that happened against your wishes, and angry about the things that did not happen according to your wishes.

If only ...

the power in
the pause

What went wrong?

Wait a minute. According to you things *could have* gone another way, but they did not, and that is what went wrong. But our question now, which needs an honest answer, is: where was the freedom of choice that went-a-begging?

Your colleagues, your competitors, and the customer, and all the factors that circumscribed the transaction, were participants in the movement, and contributors to the result. And you yourself. Each a continuity of causal flow, each a cascade of cause and consequence, each a solid fact forged on the anvil of Time to be endowed at this moment with a natural reality that nothing can deny or replace. And when these varied facts are put together and the impression of each is left upon combined action, can there be the possibility of a result other than what actually transpires? When given numbers are added up, can there be more than one right result?

We know another person through our observation of him, which we call the 'knowledge' we have of him. You 'know' your manager, and on that basis you project his role into the coming event. There is no other way we can plan, organise and execute action. Agreed. But what is so absolute, infallible, and sacrosanct about your predictions or pre-determinism? Don't you see, nobody knows anybody? All we have are opinions, surmises, and the *fact* need not tally with the *opinion*. Under the impact of his total inner personality, which is beyond even his own analytical perception in all its nuances, let alone yours, your manager acts as he *must*. We all act as we *must*, but in our error or our bravado, we construe it to be that we act as we *will*.

All the actors in our drama have played their parts. To believe that each player can write his and her script as the scene unfolds, and still produce a coherent cogent act, is to be blissfully ignorant of the natural scheme and method of enactment.

On the other hand, to know it rightly is to be able to enter into the spirit of what one has to do, and not only do it well but also enjoy the doing of it.

So what went wrong? Nothing. Nothing *ever* goes wrong. Laws do not go wrong. The law of gravity is not in error when you trip and fall. The law of gravity remained severely true and constant, both when you walked upright and when you fell. It is the same with causation.

Whether you approve of it or not, whether you are satisfied by the performance of the tasks assigned to your colleagues and assistants or feel sadly let down, whether the competitors and the customer did the expected or surprised you by their deeds, know that each one was acting true to his own nature. Nature never errs, the fruit is faithful to the seed. Upon whom shall we turn our anger, and to what purpose?

Be it repeated, we did not err in *anticipating*, we err if we change that to *demanding*. Now you are face to face with the result which is the manifested truth. Do not stand there judging its validity, instead judge the validity of your assumptions. You are a part of the movement, how can you judge the whole movement? The smaller cannot accommodate the larger.

This is the moment to *PAUSE,* and if you can, to smile. It is the pause that refreshes, if ever there was one. (Don't hold up the coke bottle!) That smile of acceptance, symbolising harmony of the individual with the totality, can revitalise you upon the instant.

Otherwise there is reaction. The result of the deal, seen as defeat and loss and failure, becomes the cause of your anger and sorrow, and clouds your faculty of clear thinking, of honest logic and rational behaviour. You may say things that hurt and humiliate or provoke people into retaliations, setting up a chain of escalating emotions and hardening attitudes. You may regret later or, even if it comes, but cannot fully undo the damage, for it is the nature of memory to linger long, specially with its wounds.

Reaction is the instant rebound of action and therefore a continuity of the action without a break. But a pause *ends* the action, and what follows is *fresh* action. In reaction you are a thing enmeshed, thrashing wildly and violently at fences closing in upon you. If there is an opening, you cannot see it. If there is the imperative need to conserve energy, you cannot contain your futile exertions. You feel you are a hunted animal, and that the hunter is Caprice, known variously as fate, destiny, ill luck, or evil stars.

Okay, I am exaggerating. You only took a sip of poison and I am accusing you of drinking a whole cup. Does that apology make you feel relieved and serve your future better? It should not, it cannot. The sip may be slow death. If fate and luck mean whimsical distortions of reason and justice, chance would be your providence and the toss of a coin can be your methodology. It is not so. There is a *Law* at work, without malevolence or benevolence, without prejudice or favour, timelessly the same. Of what concern can it be to the law that you see it or do not see it?

Your new experience has changed your perspective a little or a lot. Your present knowledge of those you knew earlier stands enhanced and altered. This reading will enter your calculations the next time around. Today is not the end of the world. There will be many more such situations where you must formulate policy, decide, lead, act. Your strategy next time will reflect your mutated mental perceptions. You must remain fresh, agile, alert and relaxed. Tenseness is memory jumping over the present in anxious anticipation. It is an attempt at a sneak-preview of the future, which is against the rules of the game. It is electrical energy dissipated as heat in a conductor that offers high resistance.

Of course be an achiever. *Rush with time.* Do not waste the present in time. Move briskly, act dynamically. Pour forth your energy where it can act, that is, into the moment that is *now* with you. That would be the way to rush with time.

But *do not rush time!* For time cannot be rushed. Time will move with its measured tread, and not all your wit or wrath, not all your pushing or pleading, will hasten it by one step.

Anxiety is your attempt at *rushing time. Activity* is rushing *with time.* That is why the pause is essential. Rushing ahead should not end up as running in circles, making it a frantic but futile exercise, expending maximum energy in a self-defeating sequence that yields the minimum benefits. *Action–reaction–action* is a closed circuit. The progress is illusory. *Action–pause–action* is the way to march ahead. It is the unimpeded flow of energy to its true purpose.

List that amongst your assets, and see what it does to your balance sheet.

10

the enemy within

Where limitation is the circumference, ego is the presiding centre. In the personal physical sense the body that you are is what is instinctively 'I' in your experience and acceptance. In the material world your possessions are 'mine' to you, the domain of your 'I'. In the mental sphere your memories, vivid or subliminal but every single one of them contributes its impression to your unfolding personality, are the circle within which you exist, by which you think, through which you act. In this the 'I' resides, and beyond is 'he', 'she', 'they' or 'it'. All that is other-ness, being other than I and mine.

I am not self-contained because I am not self-content. I *have* to transact with this other-ness. I have needs which express as my desires which in turn call for interaction, acquisition and enjoyment. This is the perpetual insatiable call of the ego sense. I have to enter the action, I cannot be an exile.

Your 'he, she, they' are all also I-centres *in themselves,* each an ego person recognised in the I-ness of oneself. All these I-concepts are operating with—or more correctly, are being operated by—the same basic urges—

THE ENEMY WITHIN

a) the *need* to be totally and enduringly happy, that is to say, complete in oneself here and now;
b) the *perception* of incompleteness because there is a felt desire for something that has not yet arrived and whose harmonious presence is a prerequisite for ending unhappiness;
c) the ego-directed *action* to bring about the result wished for.

EGO is not a bad word, at the worst it is a sad word. The sadness is for the ignorance that has replaced the truth of a total harmony with the mistaken identity of an individual in conflict with his environment, whose gain has to be the loss of others. As though happiness was a scarce commodity that cosmic supply was outstripped by continental demand! Well, how else can it seem to be, when objects are mistakenly endowed with the power to dispense happiness? For, truly, objects can be abundant or scarce but is happiness synonymous with profits and possessions? (This is a question we have asked before.)

Being egoistic is something else. It is to ignore the scheme and instead, become the schemer. It is to break the harmony of the part within the whole, and imagine that the whole can be made subservient to the part. It is to become unmindful of the momentum of cascading events in the foolish belief that your own will can flow unimpeded.

Cause and consequence, action and reaction, effort and reward, work and wage—these are not isolated blocks in terms of persons or events, but a panorama of continuous manifestation unfurled by Time upon the stage of Space. One who has the feel of this truth in oneself has a rightly restrained and wisely modulated ego centre, playing one's identifiable role in receiving and transmitting impulses of energy in a vast movement. Activity is a long train of gears in which the sprocket at a given location is being turned by the precedent ones and is turning the following ones. Even the prime mover (if you see yourself as that) is moved by the energy of fuel or power input, which in turn, acquired the capability through the processes of Nature (as when coal or oil came into being in the bowels of our earth). Each component has an honest job to perform, none less or more honest than the others, the perfection of each is essential for perfection in the total.

Egoism is often a bloated version of oneself. With a mind that has always functioned with scales of values where *big* is beautiful and *more* is happiness, it has been consistently important not only to be an achiever on those terms but also to be seen by all others as such. To assuage my own suspicions and resultant sorrows that I may be less than what I wish to be, I convince myself through repeated assertions and sympathetic justifications that I have arrived, and want everyone (and his cousin) to applaud my accomplishment. The vanity that seeks such acceptance and appreciation is the tragedy of egoism.

The fact of individuality is *ego*, but the fiction of his self-image is *egoism*. Because it is an inner fantasy, it may be far removed from what is perceived by others. The consequent rebuttal by others of one's self-esteem causes frustration which turns to anger. Reaction sets in, before the pause that could have conceded to the others their freedom to make their honest evaluation. This is the moment of pride, the moment that precedes the fall. Famous last words rise in the frothing head:

> *DO YOU KNOW WHO I AM?*
> *WHO DO YOU THINK YOU ARE?*

Next time you hear the bells of doom tolling, listen to the notes carefully—these two lines are the refrain.

Take an all-too-familiar situation. You are the Managing Director. In your wisdom you may have opted to remain single (to avoid conflict and confrontation at home), but there is no such simple solution at the factory. The labour union leader is one hulk of a fact you have to live with.

He represents the aspirations and expectations of a few hundred persons that work in your factory, because of whom your factory works. *You* are the entrepreneur who envisaged the facility where before there was only vacant land, mobilised the money to set it up, had the courage and the vision to assemble men, machines, materials and management. Without you all this could not have been.

You were needed. Equally the workforce was needed. Why, no less needed were the consumers whose assessed demand was the launching pad for your enterprise. Vast is the scheme of things always, infinitely vaster than any ego centre. Harmony in the unitary movement is justice, whose other name is love. But we do not recognise love in the severe impartiality of cosmic justice; there has to be a distorted dispensation in our favour before we can feel specially cared for, specially provided for, and *that* is love to our souls.

This wish for bias is no one's monopoly. All suffer from it, or hope to thrive on it. The managing director wants to maximise profit, the worker is sure he should be and can be paid higher wages, the consumer is convinced he should be getting better quality at a lower price. Even the government that swears to hold the price-line is out to enhance taxes, whenever and wherever.

After a spell of difficult months, when scarcity of your raw materials meant purchases at enhanced rates and yet you could not pass on the burden to the consumer in a depressed economy, there was a happy revival in all directions and buoyancy in your books and looks. Both were visible to the workers of course, and soon enough the union president came to you with that smile that surpasseth speech. Your best response of a grin could only be a glow-worm to his full moon.

The revival has just commenced, you said. Well, he said, things have been good these past three months. Not really, you countered, and anyhow before that things were terrible. True, true, he eased in, for a while they were not too good. But before that, I am glad to say times were good and now they are even better.

Facts and figures are there, and they remain as they are. In interpreting them and making projections, conclusions will vary and will naturally be tailored and twisted to suit each one's bias. Lines will be drawn at different levels, but if done in a spirit of understanding they cannot be too far apart, not beyond compromise.

When he talks, are you *listening*? Are you *looking* at what he is showing, quietly, without erecting a barrier of resentment, without mentally structuring defences? If you are, that is the welcome *pause* which permits receptivity without reaction and appraisal without anger. And often enough, the mood of one communicates with, or contaminates, the other.

Egoism has bestirred itself. You are the Managing Director, look at your education, your abilities, your status. You may or may not believe that physical bodies levitate but you are yourself the proof now that ego bodies levitate. It must be quite a squeeze inside the body when that happens, as it is happening to you now—and there is an overflow.

DO YOU KNOW WHO I AM?

The words are not spoken, they need not be. They are heard all right. They are ringing in your ears too, source of a spiralling upsurge, till you have established yourself in a mental posture that rates you ten times larger than life-size.

Even that is not enough. There is no stopping you now. He is only an employee, no matter that all the workers elected him unanimously as their president. He should know who's who. If he does not, it is high time he is told. So:

WHO DO YOU THINK YOU ARE?

This is not said aloud, either. It is a silent scream. Your eyes are more noisy, they are looking down on the pygmy from their high perch. You need to convince yourself that he is one-tenth of life-size.

There, you have set up your model, with one figure ten times reality and the other one-tenth of reality. The distortion is ten times ten, that is a hundredfold. Was it necessary? Was it sensible?

As though the damage is not enough, it is now the prerogative of Mr Union President to queer the pitch further. 'This arrogant man does not realise the power I wield in this place,' he is thinking. 'With the flick of a finger I can launch a strike. We are ready for it and we can hold out. I would have settled for half of our legitimate demands, but he thinks he can dictate to us. This fellow...'

DO YOU KNOW WHO I AM?

He has grown to ten times life-size. He is rearing to go. When the intellect is blocked by egoism, the source of inner counsel is stilled. Delusion takes over the steering as anger steps on the accelerator. It is his compulsive turn now to tell you or rather to tell you off. So:

WHO DO YOU THINK YOU ARE?

He will compress you to one-tenth your size and bottle you up. The reverse distortion has been completed, with ten times ten making a hundred again.

You compounded the situation a hundred times over, and he kept pace compounding that a hundred times over again. So now the 'situation' sits between the two of you as a monstrous 'problem', magnified 10,000 times.

Now these two gentlemen (no longer so gentle) are going to 'negotiate', 'bargain', for a 'settlement' or 'break off'.

A tragedy or a comedy! You call them 'labour problems'; they say 'management problems'. Both often mean only ego problems.

11

easy does it

Life does not come with guarantees (only watches do). Life fulfils itself in many ways. We are not saying that sweet words and gentle persuasion would have quickly and quietly settled the issue and bonhomie would have prevailed. This is not a sermon on socialism, whatever the good word has come to mean on tricky tongues. This is not a call for renunciation and sacrifice. We are still talking the hardheaded business language of profits but let us not fail to know that a posture of bravado and vanity makes one so soft-headed that one ends up deceiving and defeating oneself. An enemy outside is unnecessary.

Look at the other scenario. The union president comes into your room, by prior consent gracefully extended. Quieten your mind. There is no need for your mind to anticipate his words or imagine his hidden intentions. Why do you want to rush time? Prepare to listen, relaxed and attentive. That is the pause wherein truth can reflect.

See what is fair and possible in what he says. He speaks from an experience that is vivid and vital for him and for those whose position he represents. Respect it.

But there is another side to it too, one that you see and care for more than they do. The greater good over a longer period requires austerity and consolidation, rather than a largesse that is pleasing today but painful in the times ahead.

Now, be yourself. Do not be clever, just be honest. Honesty deals with facts whereas cleverness becomes a defence against conjured up probabilities. Tell him: 'I now see more clearly the aspects you have stressed. There are a few points that should also be weighed in, and these are more visible from my end than from yours, and therefore, it now becomes my responsibility to explain to you their implications.'

Offer to talk to all the men. Suppose your factory shift changes at 2 p.m. Consider getting both shifts to assemble at the entrance (or elsewhere) for fifteen minutes, so that you can stand amidst them informally (why not upon a stool?) and tell them: 'Your president has ably and precisely put forth your present thinking and wishes. We will discuss them further. But before that I feel there are some other factors that influence the decision, and it seems to me that you may not be sufficiently aware of them. So I want to acquaint you with those aspects, and when you and I have the complete picture in front of us, and you have had a chance to evaluate our correct overall position, your president can speak to me, or if you wish a few of you can sit with me, and let us together try to figure out what is best.'

Then tell them, simply and truthfully, what they have misunderstood or failed to reckon, and what would be better for the organisation according to you.

Do not be anxious. Suppose they do not understand ... suppose they do not believe me ... suppose they only want immediate gains ... It is not in your hands to regulate their thinking. They are so many individuals with their own moulded minds, and their collective energy will shape their response. You will know it when the response comes, and till then you have no part to play. Of course, you can worry, if that makes you feel good or great. But if you can PAUSE you stay fresh and rejuvenated to start the action when it is called for.

The chances are that your honest evaluation is heeded and the union agrees to maintain status quo for six months and review the matter then; or they feel a part of their request can be met now without straining the cash flow and the rest can wait for a more stable day. You will also not hesitate to implement reasonable benefits for them.

It is also possible that the positions on both sides remain rigid because of persisting differences in perception, or due to intransigence on either side or on both. Then what else is possible but to accept the outcome and go through with it?

Yet there is a world of difference between the stand taken *after* pursuing the path of righteousness through honesty in thought, understanding in mind, and truthfulness in action; and the same stand taken inconsiderately for selfish or egoistic ends.

Even if you have to face a strike now and destructive forces raise their heads for a while and avoidable losses are thrust upon you by a few misguided or mischievous persons, there is greater inherent strength and vitality in the organisation at the end of the unhappy episode, than could have possibly been the case if by brute authority, or clever ruse, or falsehood and deceit, you had been able to enforce an unjust decision and gain an immediate 'victory'.

For, the wise ones have proclaimed: *'He who protects righteousness, is protected by righteousness.'* One has to dive deep to plumb the depths of that declaration. You may not be in the mood for it yet, but if you can get a little feel of its import, you have changed your destiny.

To live these values, one has to shed egoism. But it is not a surrender to the other, it is a surrender to the higher potential within oneself. To acquiesce in a situation without honest conviction would be cowardice, trickery or treachery. Meek subjugation to virulent forces can be, and should be, galling, but to stand humbly before one's own conscience and face the truth as revealed therein, is real heroism. What should prevent us from doing that?

How much easier it is to live with Truth! For, truth has its own legs to stand on and does not depend on extraneous supports. But falsehood, which falsifies every support you can prop it up with, and calls again and endlessly for more and more supports, will yet collapse, for what thing can be held aloft by its shadows?

meditate... who? me?

Meditation is ... but excuse me, did I startle you by suddenly bringing in that word? I have not forgotten your suspicions of me. You have no patience with those that would nominate some unproved and unprovable supremo named GOD as the arbiter of your fate and fortune. You will have no truck with those that counsel renunciation of desire and abandonment of pleasure, and bring you for cosmetics holy ashes with which to besmear your well-groomed torso. And naturally you are suspicious that I, who professed to be your honest friend and have so far upheld your confidence by carefully avoiding any dependence on a mysterious alien, may now be preparing to trick and trip you by bringing in that God by the back door.

Otherwise, your mind is jolted into exclaiming, why do we have to talk of meditation when we are solely concerned with how to improve my balance sheet?

Easy, my friend. I am innocent till I am proved guilty, as the law concedes even to one accused of murder. So, to proceed:

Meditation is mobilising one's mental energy to achieve one's objective.

Therefore, meditation is what we are all always employing as the operative mechanism behind our actions. But we do not call it by that name, as it merits no recognition in its normal functioning. We do not say, 'that man is breathing', but when that breathing is emphasised and intensified we say, 'that man is panting'. Similarly, when the mind seems to be handled in a noticeably different and distinct manner, which becomes a necessity when the objectives call for such intensity of purpose and pursuit, it can be termed meditation.

The same demand for intensity may catch one disoriented and inadequate. It then leads to agitation which is self-destructive. We are not in that category. We have an appreciation of the rules of the kingdom, the majestic laws that no one is free to trespass without fear of penalty, and within this framework we are bravely and brightly trying to secure the best that can be rightly ours. We will not get programmed for agitation.

There are some who believe that given all the success you desire you will yet come out, then and there, with another and lengthier shopping list. They conclude that seeking to satisfy wants as a means to gain abiding contentment is as counterproductive as if, upon seeing a destructive fire that must be quelled, one splashes petrol upon it with pious belief that the fluid will put it out. They are touched by an inner intimation that the peace and beatitude, which must be the ultimate attainment of a fulfilled life, cannot be the natural corollary to enhanced profits. Their objective is to attain such lasting bliss. They too, of course, have to meditate, because, as already stated, meditation is mobilising one's mental energy to achieve one's objective. So we see them seated, quiet, often with eyes closed so that the outer vision may least disturb the inner focus. We have come to identify that scene with meditation. Leave them alone, we need not sit in judgement on them (or sit with them).

We do not belong to that category either. We are neither the confused and agitated type, nor the type that thinks a million bucks in less than ... oh, don't even say it, it hurts. We are the realists, with no apologies.

Meditation is the method for us too, for it is the honing of our energies for our own purpose, the brilliance of planning, the mastery in execution, alertness amidst changing circumstances, the iron will that seems to compel events into submission. How shall we meditate?

Your mind is the real capital that you have. Its content and texture determine your desire and action, and the pleasure or pain resulting from the action returns to the mind as experience to remain as memory. Our question therefore resolves itself into this: what state of mind will be most conducive to harnessing the full potential of your mind to your goal?

Memory is the filing section in the Department of Mental Affairs. It is there to serve your progress in life by making available to you at every stage such related material as is relevant for the present purpose. The intellect in you is the Chief Executive who studies the connected papers (files sent by memory), and takes the decision on the action to be initiated. Irrelevant or insufficient information can easily foul up the works.

Your memory is your own, true, but you do not know a mass, a totality, that you call your 'memory'. What you know is that part of your memory, a very small fragment indeed, that is *presently* brought into your awareness. From its unseen location, it has come into the field of your vision. You were here; it arrived; then you saw it. It was not yours to know and utilise till it was propelled from the dark spaces of its storage into the light of your cognition.

Your money is in the bank's vaults. Yours no doubt, but you do not walk into the vault and walk out with it (if you do that, you are an armed terrorist and the money is someone else's). There is a method, there has to be, in order to protect you and to have rhyme and reason in the whole concept of such management. Your demand is conveyed to the bank following prescribed (and mutually agreed) procedures, in response to which, and in accordance with the same procedure, the amount is made available to you in your office. Once in your hands, it is yours to deal with as you opt to. Similarly, from the vaults of memory, your collected experiences of a lifetime must be shuffled and sorted out to bring to you those items that have become relevant for the task on hand.

You see a person. For an instant it is just the *seeing,* a perception of form in your consciousness. A second later, you recognise him. It is, indeed, *re-cognition,* for you are cognising again what you had cognised before. Even if it is someone you have not seen before, or something you have not heard before, the moment it is heard or seen memory interprets it in remembered terms, and that is knowledge for you. It is with that knowledge that you proceed to plan and execute action.

Thus memory is the causal state of your mind and perceived thought is its manifestation, the effect. Cause is abstract and intangible; it is known in its modification as effect. Its existence as cause is inferred upon perceiving the effect. So you (and I) who live with the effect—more accurately, who live as the effect—have no entry into the causal frame.

Who has, then? Who is the bank manager who keeps your wealth in custody, who processes your demand and serves your need? If he is another and not you, how does he get accommodated in your mental workings where only your 'I'-ness can exist?

A good question, which whispers its own answer for he cannot be other than you, but for the present we can only see and understand this much with clarity born of personal assertable experience: he is *NOT* you *as you now know yourself*. If you and he share an identity in a recast frame of a higher truth, that is beyond the scope of our present pursuit, then let us continue on the basis that we cannot manipulate memory though we are dependent upon memory for our efficiency.

In this light, look upon the standard admonition to concentrate, to command memory to place before you ... what? If you know what, you do not need further service from memory, and if you do not know what, what will you ask of memory?

The best course you can follow is to *BE QUIET*. It is the *PAUSE* that turns productive. Memory is a good servant but a bad master. When you attempt to instruct memory, you only reveal your ignorance and ineptitude. Memory chuckles to itself feeling deservedly superior, and with roles reversed, toys with you; whereas, if you had waited with quiet dignity, memory as your bounden slave would have garnered the relevant details and waited upon your sweet pleasure. Your felt desire, quietly held, is command enough to your memory.

You see, what you circumscribe as your memory, keeping your ego-person as the centre of that circle, is not really an isolated island. Consciousness is a unitary vastness, as space is. With what will you isolate an area of space? Oh, that is easy, you say, with four walls I create a room space. True, you say this is the inside of the room within the four walls, and beyond is the outside. But where are the walls resting even now? Are they not in space, even now? If the walls are now removed, would you have to shovel in space to fill a spacelessness? So if inside is space—the walls are in space, and the outside is space—is the division of space a mental illusion or a physical fact?

Similarly, whatever you conjure up, or conceive of, as a limitation to consciousness is a *known* thing, a point of knowledge, a construct of consciousness, which means in other words that it is a content of consciousness. Where then is the limitation of a container? To hold water you need a vessel. The vessel cannot be made of water. It has to be something else like a metal. There is nothing other than consciousness to be fashioned into a container of thoughts which themselves constitute consciousness. What is infinite has no limitation. Consciousness, like space, is all-pervasive.

If that is understood, it follows that the operation of the energy of consciousness is also a unitary movement that cannot be limited by parameters of space or time. Its flow is 'causation' engulfing the whole of humanity in a cascade of cause–effect. Nothing can be unknown to the knowing principle which consciousness is, so evidently, no data is missed in its reckonings. It is the cosmic computer that cannot go wrong. And what is implemented is an unfailing law. Perfect administration of accepted law is justice, is it not? How can we honourably ask for anything else, or ever think that it can be bettered?

The best we can do is to stop imagining that our initiative is called for and that our inputs will enhance or hasten the results. Any interference from the ego centre that vainly arrogates to itself a private source of energy, will only result in the ego dissipating the share of energy it is allotted from the central pool, depriving itself of the chance in good time to put it to productive use. A good citizen obeys the law, he does not go around structuring it. *He need not.*

So we have to know what that meditative poise is. You remember we tip-toed away from one who was sitting motionless with eyes closed? Well, his purpose, in pursuit of the goal of total freedom from desire, was to close the mind too. Our purpose is different. It is to open the mind, to enable the mind to function at its highest potential. Just the same, it helps us also to know when to close the eyes. And to stay still for a while, so that the quietening of the body, the withdrawal from perceiving the external world, may leave us silently with ourselves. Let thoughts be stilled, the thoughts that conjure up many possibilities, whereas only one result is possible, that result which is the rightful law-abiding effect of the existing cause. Let that effect reveal itself to you. You have no action to perform to make that happen. Be in harmony with the law and let it work for you.

While you wait thus, awake and inactive, you will see the action as it is meant to be. You will see it with clarity and appreciation, and can therefore, enter into the action with assurance and even joy, because you are in harmony with the movement and that harmony is the music of the mind.

It is not that one sits in meditation for a determined time and alternates it with periods when he jumps into activity. When the approach becomes a way of life, both coexist. *There is an inner quietude even while there is an outer dynamism. That is action without reaction.* That is life's energy focused upon itself and fulfilling itself in its grandest enactment.

13

doership

When we can thus behold the sweep and majesty of the tidal movement in the expanse of consciousness, that each of us, of individual mind, experiences as personal action and result, where, in it, shall be located our sense of doership?

For you say, it has always been my unambiguous gut-sense, my vivid primal experience, that I myself *will* my actions and I execute them. Whatever may be the theoretical rationale of a total unitary upsurge, I seem to choose the time and method of my action and launch it. If I am not the doer of what I do, who else is? How absurd can we get?

Step wary, my friend. He who walks along the peaks must step gingerly, for it is easy to slip there. In the foothills a slip may mean bruises or at worst a broken toe, but in the dizzy heights of mountains death is only one false step away. Yet the lure of adventure and achievement takes men high among the towering cliffs when heroism beckons.

We are talking of heroic deeds today. Not content with average performance and mediocre profits, we are penetrating the deeper recesses of life-energy to harness it to our greater ambition. Naturally in the process, the easy beliefs of a habituated mind will come apart, common understanding will turn complex and complex sequences will reveal the simple secret of their arrangement, and words like knowing and doing and being will break their crusty shells of dull usage to emerge as powerful beacons of a new awakening.

Your question is admitted. That you ask it is fair. Now listen carefully.

As long as you do not question the first premise of an ego-centred individuality, your description of yourself has to stand and has to be accommodated. Remember that other one of closed eyes, in meditation? Well, his mind had taken a different turn. '*WHO AM I?*' was his quest, in great earnest. His riddle was: 'This body of mine is only matter, an agglomerate of the essence of the food I consume. The real me is the consciousness that I possess, my mental activity that uses my body as its instrument. But my mind cannot be a closed circle. Can I pour a bowl of water upon the surface of the sea and say "*within the line I have drawn is my portion of the sea?*" How then can my mind be de-marked and de-linked from the boundless expanse of consciousness? In truth, "I" must be the inheritor and possessor of the indivisible totality. My perception of myself is faulty.'

And his meditation is to see whether in the stillness of his mind unruffled by thought, the Reality will reflect. He seeks no fruition of desire outside himself, he is introverted. *His sorrow* is that he has not yet discovered the lofty truth of himself; not that he hasn't gained a larger slice of the universe.

Our sorrow is that we have not made our millions yet (through honest means, no doubt) and our concern lies there. So the need to shape our destiny calls for aggressive doership. May we succeed! The happiness that we have promised ourselves must be ours to keep and cherish for ever thereafter. May it be so.

But the perception has to be right. Only then can the method be right and the resultant action productive.

Agreed that it appears that action is starting in the freedom of my will. But what seems to be, need not be. The blue in the sky, the speaker in the echo, the image behind the mirror, the water in the mirage, the event in the dream: is that not a sufficient narration to assert that what seems to be need not be?

You flick the switch and the light comes on. There is the visible linkage of action and effect, the sequence of cause and effect. Because of that, shall the switch claim doership, saying 'from me came the power that lit the bulb?' Beyond the switch and the transformer and the generator and turbine, and yet beyond as the kinetic energy in the hydel system or the thermal energy in the boiler, recedes the causal connection. But, who will deny that turning the switch on was what made the bulb glow?

So it is with us. Let us live and act in consonance with this right understanding. Then we do not bear upon our backs an assumed burden that contributes nothing to the result (except a backache).

An ignorant villager who had always walked from one place to another carrying his possessions upon his head, one day boarded a train. He sat down in it, but would not place the trunk upon the floor. He still carried it on his head!

It is no one's contention that he can leave the box unattended altogether, and take a stroll at every station, or forget all about it and expect it to be delivered at his home. All that is said is: the train will carry the burden. While sitting in the compartment, even if you place the trunk on your head, the train is still carrying the burden.

You are doing a good turn neither to yourself, nor to the train, by your kindly concern to carry your burden yourself. It is an act of doership that has consumed energy without contributing to the result.

If we are honest, we will catch ourselves acting like that villager in the train. Use the power and the momentum of the mighty locomotive, which is consciousness in movement, to haul your desires to their destination while you function deliberately within the limits of your individuality to protect and fashion your goals, even as the passenger on the train still retains responsibility for his goods. Then your energy is well conserved and utilised. Personal doership cannot scale greater heights.

14

sharing the spoils

It is quite simple.

You are *here*; that is to say, you are and can only be, in the 'here'. Your sense of 'there' is not the result of your being 'there', for where you are is 'here' for you. So it is only a mental projection from the centre moored 'here', and when you are thinking of that 'there', the knowledge of it is only 'here' where you are. That is how the mind perceives space, in the immediacy of your presence, in the dot of space wherein your I-ness is.

So is it with time too. Whatever you *know* is now, that is in the instant of that knowing. You say: I know (remember) what happened yesterday. Yes, but you know it now. The thought of that past movement was not with you today, and then in a trice it was with you, and that togetherness of you and the thought was in the *now* of its occurrence. The 'then' of the past is cognised only in the 'now' of your instant presence. Similarly, the 'future' figures in your mind when the thought of a tomorrow arises in you, but that thinking is *now* and now alone.

So the whole of infinite space, and the whole of eternal time, have reality in the locus of the perceiving 'I', and thus the macrocosm is held in the microcosmic point that you take yourself to be, *here and now*.

That is the centre of your world of happenings and any action you perform must fit this construct of mind–space–time.

You are now poised for action. The scenario is whatever it is at this moment. Freeze the frame for a minute. Look at it. Either you like it or you do not like it, but you cannot wish it away or wish it different. It is the reality of this instant in the continuity of all the causes that have shaped it. You may have been one of them, one amongst many, and whatever you did also contributed to its present form and texture. You cannot undo *now* what you did then; how much less can you think of undoing what others did!

So stand poised for action, but first stand still before the frozen frame, *ACCEPTING THE FACT* without demur.

YOU CANNOT CHOOSE THE PRESENT, YOU CAN ONLY DEAL WITH IT.

Before your action starts, let us get one more thing straight. You are also a product of the same system. The same limitation through continuity defines you too. It is all one movement.

YOU ARE PART OF THE ACTION. Now you can start acting, but do not imagine you wrote the script.

Freeze, over. Time moves again. Action. Go ahead, play your role as you will, bring into it your own nuances, your intonations, your gestures, your characteristic slant and emphasis. But remember: Sir Lawrence Oliver brought glory and renown to his performance of *Hamlet*, but the script was exactly what dear old Shakespeare wrote.

So far you are doing all right. That you had a certain legitimate desire was your business, no one else's. That you want that desire fulfilled now, fits in naturally with your progress through life. You do the best you can to attain success—fair enough. You have a hope that the result will be as you strove to make it, that your desire will be satisfied. Who can fault you for hoping so?

A famous scriptural text, in its most celebrated dictum says: 'To action you have a right, but not to the fruit thereof' (Bhagawad Gita, Ch.II sloka 47). Some wise men and many wise guys will gladly misinterpret it for you, saying that it is the supine attitude of servile humans who will mortgage their souls to an unknown Superior Being, and are held in mental slavery by being beguiled into believing this gibberish: that men shall labour but be denied of their wages. Cease not to work, stop not to reap. Capitalism at its diabolical worst, derived straight by quoting heavenly authority ...

What it means is something else, something that sets the perspective right, the rules straight, ensures that the game is played according to accepted rules for the enjoyment of all the players, for how can a team participate in a game if the rules are not known, or they are known but disregarded?

What it means is: you are aware of a certain freedom of action in *yourself*, and of your ability to launch that action at your choosing. This is a right that you recognise and wield in yourself. But do not imagine that you have the same felicity with regard to the fruits of action, for however deep and desperate your longing for them, they have been fashioned or produced *by the total action* that involves many more contributory efforts and ambitions besides your own. The fruits may be few or plentiful, they may be the sweet ones of success or even the bitter ones of failure. You cannot lunge for them and grab them. The total law will preside over the prize distribution, and with computerised accuracy the fruits will reach each participant in the action in right proportion. So you should not assume a right to the fruits, even if you indulge your inherent right to action.

Your are a little anxious, thinking, how will I get to be the millionaire I want to be if I have to accept the crumbs of some equalising benevolence? But who said you will be offered the crumbs? As likely, the cream is yours. It all depends on the overall set-up of the unfolding panorama, where you have slotted yourself (as it seems to you) or been slotted (as is more true) in the total configuration of geographical, historical, economical and political dispensations which you cannot manipulate but which largely manipulate you; and amidst this ocean of circumstances, how with courage, skill and sinew you navigate the boat of your personal determinism.

Out of this equation of the individual relating with the total, comes the quotient which determines his gain or loss. In the long story of humanity there have always been emperors and slaves. Millionaires are not a proscribed breed, nor are they an endangered species, but to be a millionaire there has to be a deserving beyond the easy desiring.

what is your problem?

You are holding your head in your cupped hands. The story is told by the very gesture. No friend asks you then 'Do you have a problem?' because your posture proclaims you have. The question asked is 'What is your problem?'

We will modify that further and ask: 'What is a problem?' Never mind the specifics of what is troubling you, but when does anyone say he has a problem?

Obviously, as long as your desires are being fulfilled, your wants satiated, and nothing is moving contrary to your wishes, there is no problem, is there? But when your personal gratification is denied, your pursuit is foiled, your effort is resisted, and the fruit you long to enjoy is plucked from your outstretched fingers or placed altogether beyond your reach, that is a problem.

Who says so? You say so.

Passing time brings about an endless array of events. One after another they approach, they stand facing you and faced by you, they recede yielding place to the next in the procession. To an objective observer, they are all so many *situations,* which on careful study indicate the possibilities of action in furtherance of an identified goal.

But to you the present situation is a *problem* because it is not shaping the way *you* wanted it to be.

My dear man, it is shaping the only way it can, given the subjugation of effect to cause, given the compulsion of the law of manifestation, given the precedent and prevailing forces that have produced their natural result. And you dare stand there and assert that all this mighty majesty of the law should be set aside, and an irrelevance that has your wish as its only support should be enthroned? What is at fault, the law's working, or your poor appreciation of reality? No happening goes awry or amiss, for it is impossible for a law to err. It is only the mind of man that brings itself to think that such an error has taken place. So MAN **HAS** NO PROBLEM, MAN HIMSELF **IS** THE PROBLEM.

You are a reasonable man—when it comes to advising the neighbour. But when you are chasing results on which you have decided your happiness hinges, your reason is distorted, your vision is clouded, you are ready to kick the world around. The world will not budge an iota in its orbit, and you will stub your toe or shatter your foot. Dispassion about the future right now, even while you pour passionate energy into present action, is the secret of diligent doership.

Nature has no anxiety about the unnatural! But man, who proclaims himself the supreme perfection of evolutionary intelligence, talks of unnatural 'calamities' such as floods, tidal waves, earthquakes, and 'accidents' such as planes crashing and mines collapsing. If there is anything unnatural in creation, it is the idea of the unnatural in the mind of man.

Water flows down a gradient, water finds its level. These are basic laws, and there is nothing that water *can* do about them. There is nothing that water *wants* to do about them either. Torrential rains all around, sustained for several days, exceed all your expectations which are based on past averages and your lovely home is flooded. It is a devastating sight. Your sorrow is understandable, your sense of loss invokes our sympathy. But to accuse nature of malice or misbehaviour, and to harbour resentment and rancour at unidentified evil intentions plotting your agony, would amount to less than common sense. Acting diligently to salvage what can still be saved of your possessions would be much more to the point and to your profit.

There are no *accidents,* there are only *happenings,* all always expressing the unwavering law that manifests causes as effects. Suddenly on a flight something goes wrong—wrong in the sense that one did not expect it then. One did not expect it then because one did not know how the related causal factor was shaping. A stress had been developing, a hairline crack had appeared in the structure and had been imperceptibly but unrelentingly widening. At one instant of metal fatigue, calculable if all the data was available, a section of the plane's wing fell off. The plane crashed. Eighty-two persons were killed. Three survived with burns and injuries. One of those that died was a poor *'unlucky'* farmer who was on his land into which the debris fell.

... And there was the lucky one who got caught in the traffic jam and missed the flight and went home to go

And there was that *'lucky'* one (thank God—never mind which God) who missed the flight because he got into a traffic jam and went home to get the news on TV.

Death we accept as natural to all life. *'Mors certa, hora incerta.'* Death is most certain, the time of death is most uncertain. We know someone or the other is dying each passing day. Tell me, is there more death when a hundred die than when one dies, or when a hundred die together at one place than when a hundred have died individually all over the world at that same time? Can there be a reckoning, as it were, of hundred times death, that enhances the intensity or the finality of the fact of death?

The mind of man says: 'Dying is natural, but dying like this is unnatural.' No great harm that you use one word or the other; but that thinking surreptitiously seeps into our beliefs and shapes our attitudes. At the core level of our operating psychology we retain the distorted and disastrous sense that the law is inconsistent and is therefore no law at all. Thereby we concede that normal events are one thing, accidents are another. Causation is one thing, luck is something else.

And when there is no Law, the sanity and sanctity of cause–effect relationship is denied, and *CHANCE* becomes the logic of dispensations. Then, where is direction to planning and dynamism to purpose?

That is why it becomes important to know that nothing happens that should not have happened, and nothing will fail to happen that should happen, inasmuch as cause *WILL* manifest as effect, and without cause there *CANNOT* be an effect.

The congregation of exactly those travellers on the flight, the traffic jam that had many irritated and inconvenienced participants (to us unnamed and unsung) whose cumulative demeanour was to result in saving the

WHAT IS YOUR PROBLEM?

life of the 'lucky' one (named and sung), the seemingly detached unrelated farmer upon the ground working there at that instant—all of this, and also that while so many were crushed to mangled death a few survived—it is all one moment of rightness and nothing but rightness to each and every participant in the total action.

This is not 'fatalism', it is the superior perception of fact, the essence of underlying order seen in superficially disconnected events. That is why problems do not exist in the whole chronicle of unfolding time; they exist only in the mental attitude of man.

Now will you uncup your hands, lift up your head, smile, and look the event straight in the eye?

16

the ultimate economy

Thoughts are experienced one at a time because each thought must receive attention to register itself in consciousness, but their succession in rapid flow creates the impression of unbroken continuity, and we aver that mind is thought flow. It is exactly as the intermittent projection of one frame after another from the cinematographic reel of film gives us the impression of continuous action upon the screen; or the rapid twirling of a flaming torch creates the vision of a circle of fire. Know that to be the methodology of mental discernment.

When similar thoughts are grouped together, the mind dwells on one subject for a while. As a man of action, you will have a few, or even several, subjects pending decision and disposal at your hands on any morning. You may determine the order of priority, but evidently, you have to deal with one subject at a time. You have to process or finish the matter as thoroughly as is possible, and move on to another.

But what happens most of the time? You consider the action and see possible blocks or delays, or gaps in required information. You become agitated. You may become angry.

THE ULTIMATE ECONOMY 75

Both mental states mean that the rate of thought flow has risen steeply. They are not productive and they further reduce your ability to make clear decisions, but who is to tell you that then?

You are wasting time. You are wasting energy, but your ego-sense is being pampered by that posture of confronting the world, and there is vicarious satisfaction in that.

Your frisky mind flits from one subject to another, nibbling at each but consuming none.

That is no way to function. You are aware of many areas of manpower and material management and money flow where economies must be identified and enforced, but are you aware that *ECONOMY OF THOUGHT* has precedence over all else if your balance sheet should read better?

Thought is the energy that deals with all other energies that work for you. Give to each task the thought it needs *and no more*. *CONSERVE THOUGHT* and your real capital is intact. When your alert mind is still, quiet, reined in, it is not wasting time, but in fact has made time itself wait upon your command. Your efficiency is at a peak.

If you are not agitated, does it signify that you are not inspired? Aggressiveness stemming from confusion and indiscretion will not hasten or help the action in positive terms, but will only lead to resentment, conflict and disharmony. On the other hand, the calmness of a steadied mind sees the plan of action step by step, guides the participants clearly, and creates the most favourable environment for success.

You may object, saying: 'You get nowhere if you are not aggressive. You have to demand results. Perform or quit. You have to reprimand the inefficient, you have to punish the troublemaker, you have to layoff the surplus. Being soft does not take you far. I do not run a charity home.'

Take such action if you have to. Of course there are norms to be followed, and a sense of fair play is not charity. Beyond that, let the punishment suit the crime. But where is the call for agitation? Let the angry look show in your eyes, let the firm words in a slightly raised voice (please do not shout) reveal your disapproval, and pronounce what you must. Let it all be from the neck upwards. Why should it originate from your belly, with the bile flowing and the insides churned up and the abdominal muscles all tensed up? How does it help you or your victim?

It does not help. How and whether it hurts the other is not our present concern, but we have to see how it hurts you. We have seen it already in your doctor's advice. 'Blood-pressure is somewhat high,' he says in cautious understatement which translates into: You are not dead yet, but you are trying. 'Hyperacidity' he adds succinctly, meaning your stomach is a hydrochloric acid plant, and production in that factory is good (whatever the production be in your other factory). You are asked to stay on a low-salt, low-fat diet ... and 'I need not tell you this—stay off drinks'. (But damn it all, doctor, this is just when I need a drink because I am agitated.)

It is almost funny, the way we call them 'heart attacks'. That poor old faithful organ, a soft tender pulsating mass hardly the size of one's fist, charged with the duty of working, without ceasing for a minute, from the instant of birth (even earlier) to kingdom is mercilessly teased and tormented by inputs of food and impulses of moods that would demolish a fortress, and if having borne it all heroically for years, it finally succumbs to the accumulated insult and injustice, and even then does not fall but only falters—you call *THAT* a heart attack! For shame, there is never a heart attack on man, there is only a *man-attack* on the heart! The heart deserves our gratitude, not our accusation.

They tell the story of a big serpent that dwelt in the grasslands of an Indian hamlet. Being of a nasty temper, it would get provoked for no greater reason than that the cowherd boys played upon the cool slopes, and it would chase them with an intention to bite. The boys were lucky to escape on fast heels or else would have fallen prey to it.

A saintly man was passing that way one day and he saw this happen. After the boys had fled, by the power of his austerities and a soul thus purified, he was able to summon the snake to his presence and communicate with it. He admonished the snake for its unjustifiable and destructive behaviour, and advised it to change its ways. He explained it all to the snake and left saying that he would return that way after two weeks and would like to have a progress report from it.

The snake was deeply touched by the loving goodness of the mendicant and its nature soon became docile. The boys would now catch sight of its gleaming torso in the sunlight and by instinct retract a pace, but seeing that it did not move, advance a little as boys do, and watch. Then they would shout. Then they would throw stones. Still the snake lay still. Growing bolder by degrees, the bravest amongst the lads quickly grasped the serpent by its tail, whirled it in the air and dashed it against the ground. Then, taking no further chances, the boys ran home in glee.

The snake lay there bruised and battered. It could not get its food and was famished. Still it accepted everything as the meaning and method of a virtuous life and suffered without complaint.

It was then the saintly man returned. He called for the snake. It could hardly crawl to where he was and pay its obeisance. 'What is the matter?' he said, in sad surprise. The gentle snake would not blame anyone. 'Nothing Master, I just happened to hurt myself amidst some boulders.' But the saint was not to be deceived. He surmised the facts.

He said '*oh you lovable idiot. I told you not to bite and inject your deadly venom into the boys. Did I tell you not to hiss?*' If the snake had just raised its head and hissed, the offending boys would have fled the scene and the snake could have laughed (if snakes laugh). No harm would have been done to anyone, yet all constructive purposes would have been fully served.

There is often an adequate measure between the extremes. If you don't bite, it does not mean you have to kiss. Just hiss-s-s.

at the crossroads

TRUST YOURSELF. This is not an option, this is the only way everyone operates at all times. When you say 'I trust you' you are saying *'I trust the veracity of my conclusion that I may trust you.'* We have to keep coming back to this in any attempt at right understanding of the basics—that everything is contained in 'experience' alone, and all experience is contained in 'I-ness' alone. Trust has no centre other than oneself.

You ask: Then why do you have to tell me *'Trust yourself'*? To bring the unconscious methodology of mental workings into your conscious focus, not because that alters the fact in any way, but because it clears misconceptions that deny you the positive strength that the truth can bestow upon you.

Often in your role of decision-maker you find yourself with viable alternatives and have to take one path to the exclusion of others (as you cannot be in two places at one time). This then is the scenario. On your arduous journey by car through an expanse of rather unfrequented terrain, you have arrived at crossroads. You know of course the name of the town that is your destination, but you do not know which way to go from this point.

Fortunately, there is a signpost there and the arm that points to the right bears the name of the place you wish to reach. Lesser mortals may accept that as the final commandment, but you are a prudent man, a cautious man.

Suppose the illiterate labourers who fix these posts in arid stretches, had made a mistake? Then the pointer could be off the mark, and where would you be if you just took it on trust? Then again, these are days when unruly boys do anything for kicks. Suppose a gang of such kids had turned the signpost a neat ninety degrees, and were even now hiding behind distant bushes to see you make a fool of yourself? You are too clever for them. They will have to wait, and yours will be the last laugh. So you wait there, reciting the virtues of patience. Luck favours the brave, so a bus is seen coming the way you came. You observe diligently and read clearly that the panel in front has the legend of the destination of the bus, and it is the same as your wonted destination. The bus slows down, turns right, and goes its way.

Sufficient confirmation to common folk, but you are intelligent. Suppose the name-board on the bus had been wrongly hung at the bus depot, or ... why not? We should not ignore possibilities ... judgements must follow exhaustive investigation ... suppose that bus driver was new on this route, and did not know the roads, and did not have your wisdom to be sure before he turned?

My friend, in that case, from then on your address will be 'care of signpost, crossroads, no-man's land.' And may you grow roots standing there!

Sir, it is better to decide and walk any path rather than stand unto eternity hugging the signpost. Even if

AT THE CROSSROADS

you make a mistake (you decided the left turn looked better) and go as far as you have to, to be told at the next village, or anywhere and anyhow be corrected, and then have to retrace your steps to the old crossroads, now to take the right turn (which is the right turn), by this action, and elimination, you would have made progress towards reaching your destination.

Life comes with no guarantees (unlike watches. You heard that before) and no peeping Tom upon his toes has yet looked over the wall of 'now' into a 'tomorrow'. You have to act and await results and act further. To block action with overanxiety is to defeat yourself. The old English proverb seems to have been only one-half written (rather foolishly)—in full it should have read: *'Fools rush in where angels fear to tread, and they thus become wiser.'* Better that than be a fool for ever.

One can say it either way. Do they not also say: *'Nothing venture, nothing gain'* or *'fortune favours the brave'*? Any generalisation is a half-truth. The full truth you can aspire to is to be true to yourself. And to be that is to trust yourself.

When you trust yourself you are self-confident and are therefore relaxed. *Relaxation* is the springboard of efficiency, not what is normally termed and understood as concentration. *Concentration* is an assertion of will, and *will* is the thrust of intelligence, and intelligence is the total of the known. If you decide that you need to recollect some information to formulate your course of action, obviously that data needs recall from wherever it lies unknown to you at this moment, and tell me how your will is going to enter that walled fortress of the unconscious and ferret out the information for you.

As we have seen all along, that is the area of the causal state, which remains unmanifest till it is revealed to your intellect as a thought which is the effect, and which sprouts out true to the seed that gives it birth. When you are possessed of the knowledge, you can use it and deal with it. There is no need then to flex your mental muscle and clench your fists. Any stress you introduce will be your deluded effort to operate upon cause—how can you while you are its offspring and cause is the parent?—and the only result can be that you introduce counter-eddies into what would have otherwise been a smooth flow.

Memory, let it be repeated, is a good servant. The facts stored therein are yours by right of past acquisition. All of them are not required by you all the time. If, the moment memory's door is opened, all the contents came tumbling out, you will be engulfed under a mountain of miscellany. If you are thirsty for a drink of water, you do not want a whole river to be diverted into your throat. Sensible management of the store consists of your having access

AT THE CROSSROADS

to *what* you need *when* you need it. In a relaxed yet alert mind, that is what happens.

Then relevant data is processed, put together, and presented to you. Your strain of will which is an ill-conceived attempt to compel and hasten the natural process, only succeeds in sending self-contradictory messages to the dutiful mind, confusing its rhythm and setting up blocks.

A relaxed mind is an unconditioned mind, emptied of the unwanted and therefore ready to receive the wanted. It is a mind ever brimming with energy, because it expends so little of it, being skilled in achieving effortlessly.

mind is relativity

Do not look for the ultimates; ultimate achievement or success or efficiency or obedience or anything else. The *absolute* does not reside in the kingdom of the *relative*. The mind of man talks about the absolute without knowing what it is talking about. Everything the mind knows is within the realm of relativity. The mind formulates all its concepts in terms of pairs of opposites, and so is for ever poised between happiness and unhappiness. All life's experiences are defined mentally as good or evil, pleasant or unpleasant, honourable or dishonourable, virtuous or sinful, elevating or degrading, lovable or hateful; physically as heat or cold, hard or soft, tasty or bitter, big or small, fragrant or foul. Each one of these concepts forms a linear scale, but it is not a line with a midway mark, to one side of which is the 'positive' value, and to the other side the 'negative'. At any point along the line, the opposites lie on either side. When is one rich? When one has only a thousand, ten thousand is rich; but when one has arrived at ten thousand, only hundred thousand can convey the feel of being rich. And if that is granted, the longing is for a million. At that time the cause of sorrow is the fact of possessing 'a hundred thousand only'.

Thus the value of everything in the field of relativity is a mental disposition, a factor dependent upon the mental state and propensities of the individual. The mind knows nothing of anything that is not relative, and so concepts like status and superiority have no constant base. This mind which cannot transcend relativity, and so cannot have a concept outside a pair of opposites, plays foolishly at exceeding itself, and tricks itself into a verbal assertion of an absolute by coining that word, as though by a mental construction it can delink itself from its foundations. Such an absolute is only part of another (if final) pair where the idea of 'relative' is opposed to the idea of 'absolute'.

The importance of appreciating this is that you can then remain fresh and flexible. You can willingly give up the rigid posture of determining what is right and arrogating to your judgement a finality that all the world should recognise. In the relative workings of minds, honest difference of opinion and conclusion is natural. When you can see and accept that as a fact of life, you can work free of debilitating resentment and instead use your energies to steer clear of obstacles or climb over them. When you do not see it, you will be butting a blank wall with your head, instead of walking round it and beyond.

We live in a universe of constant and compulsive changes. Our earth itself is rotating on its axis (which too shifts its angle) and also revolving round the sun. Where then is stillness or rest for anything or anyone? In the individual's body, every single cell perishes progressively and gets replaced, so that they say after a lapse of twelve years there is not one cell left which was there at the start—so what are you talking of the same person being there? In every atom in creation there is a gyrating whirlpool of constant motion—then what is meant by stationary object? And in the mind of man there is a rapid unending flow of thoughts, and at any moment man is what his thought is—so what is he in constant terms?

At least space and time are constants, we believed, as long as three dimensional space of classical Euclidean geometry contained Newton's mechanical model of the universe. Our physics rested there for centuries. But *TIME* changed all that—in more senses than one! For time revealed itself as 'the fourth dimension' of space. Whatever sense that makes, it does not make common sense, so you and I will opt out of the discussion and leave it to the physicists—but you and I too have to note now, even more emphatically, that what we were saying earlier is in fact truer than we claimed. When science too says that space is not unchangeable and time is not uniform, then what is absolute reality to the mind?

We are talking of abiding happiness as the goal of striving humanity, our personal conviction being that the perfected company balance sheet is a synonym for it. In the vast realm of relativity there are many paths to the destination.

"Don't bother where I am Just tell me how to go to where you are!"

Now, you are getting a long-distance call. It is your good long lost friend and a jolly fellow from college days.

'How are you?'

'Fine. I have been hopping around the country, I want to see you. How do I get there?'

You are sitting in your small-town office. You say, 'Just tell me where you are and ...'

'Don't bother about where I am. Just tell me how to get to where you are.'

Is that not crazy? What directions are possible? Without knowing exactly where he is, can I chart his journey to a destination? Similarly, without knowing my own mental composition and the equilibrium of the various forces operating therein, how efficiently and realistically can I plan my life's voyage? I should know my present location.

In this kaleidoscope that seems to you to be an endless flux of chance and change, wherein you and your desires and your capabilities are for ever varying, wherein the charm and attraction attributed to objects is not constant, wherein all the people around you that you have to relate to and transact with, are as prone to change as you are—in all this whirl, how can there be pre-drawn lines along which you can guide your footsteps securely?

To demand such security or to believe that it can be had, would be to live unwisely, because it would be asking for the absolute within the relative. On the other hand, to be free in the mind and open to what each moment unfolds, to greet it with wonder without confusion, and joy without anxiety, would be utilising your potential to perfection.

To do so, first accept the truth of what you are. Know where you are. See yourself honestly as you are now. And that knowledge will effortlessly fashion the harmony with the movement, rather within the movement. That is all the security that one needs or can aspire for.

one thing at a time

You say: 'I am up to my neck in work today.' May be true. But there is nothing desperate in that situation. It calls for steady wisdom, application and organised effort. With that you will emerge from being neck-deep till you can wade out on firm feet. But now, just when your integrated intelligence should be at its brightest, you (normally a man of impeccable judgement) have become anxious. Agitation is building up, drawing upon itself for nourishment. Though the flood level has in no way increased, you find your nose submerged, solely because of the posture into which you have sunk. Now, a manageable situation has been needlessly rendered catastrophic, and well may you drown, without even realising that you were not murdered, you committed suicide.

No matter how high the pile of files upon your polished executive desk, you can only deal with one subject at a time. You may determine your order of priority with some personal freedom and preference, but the law of nature lays down that you can deal only with one subject at a time.

A river is a flood of water in constant motion, and if standing upon the bank you let your gaze take in the visible stretch, there is a moving mass of churning waters in endless flow. But at a point of fixed sight straight in front of you, instant by instant, there is only that limited defined quantity of water. The flow is a continuity of change, but the change is of one unit to another unit to yet another unit, an intermittent process of renewal. The experience for the witness upon the bank is of a flowing river and the river has acquired an identity, but the truth at the point and time of instant observation was drop ... drop ... drop.

Mind is consciousness in movement, a flow of thoughts. Like a river it seems to have an undifferentiated continuity, but whether a trickle or a flood, it is thought ... thought ... thought.

One more simile will not hurt us—not when the point is of cardinal importance. Recall the silver screen. (Hope you took your wife to the movies last Sunday?) Remember the sweep and swing of the action. But in truth was it not one picture frame at a time that lingered a fraction of a second upon the screen, disappearing to yield place to another and again another? Yet what disappeared from the orbit of ocular vision was preserved in mental vision, and linked together in mental mechanics though not in real optical terms, to create an experience of continuity.

The point we need to establish is that the inexorable and inevitable operation of the mental mode is to contain only one thought at a time, no more and no less. Rapidity of succession does not alter the basic law. To be clearly aware of this is to be in harmony with and therefore attuned to, the possibilities and limitations of one's energy, and such clear perception is the bestower of efficiency.

Now we are ready for action. Take up the first matter to be dealt with. Hope there is the semblance of a smile upon your lips, not of arrogance or superiority, not of teaching someone a lesson or of showing someone his place, but merely a suggestion of the joy of living, of the exhilaration of a new day offering an opportunity to put varied factors together into their harmonious relationships to discover the total truth existing in them already, but presently hidden from your knowledge.

Give it all your attention. The hallmark of such undivided attention is relaxation, freedom from strain. To see what is, as it is, cannot be a strain. Strain is when memory intercedes too fast, interpreting, projecting, demanding and doubting. They are all so many thoughts and they have taken over the screen, pushing aside the thought of factual observation-in-the-present. So where are you when that happens? Anywhere but where you should be, and worse, where you fondly imagine that you indeed are. A destructive flood of mental activity has enslaved you, wasting your energy, wasting your time, and defeating your purpose. In the misguided notion of doing more, you are doing less. Imagining you are aggressive against factors external, you have turned aggressive against yourself internally.

You will *have* to return to the thought that you weakly allowed to be sidelined, and hold it again in the focus of your attention to the exclusion of others, for there is no other way you can deal with it. Do you have to do it after all the wasted energy and wasted time? Why did you not stay unmoved in the first instance?

An agitated mind is defenceless against the onslaught of memory. It is only a calm mind that is the master of its resources which rest in the vaults of its memory, ready to serve when commanded. When the present revelation of new facts has been properly cognised, memory shall be summoned to evaluate and structure the data into utilitarian action. But if memory jumps the gun and shatters the peace of quiet observation, it is an exercise in futility. *THE CALM MIND CREATES; THE FURIOUS MIND FRUSTRATES.* Jumping frantically where you stand is not running a race; the race is run with fluent strides that flow in purposeful harmony, each a swift execution of undeterred agility.

That is the way the mind should function in running the race against accumulating workload.

afraid of what?

Fear is the insignia of limitation.

I am limited, as a person; and I need to go beyond the present limits by reaching out into the world outside in terms of expression, action, acquisition and achievement. That urge is the felt desire, the innate intimation of an incompleteness in myself as I am, the inner conviction that my happiness remains dented till the fulfilment of the immediate desire. It is the call for action.

But I also know that all the elements of 'otherness' around me, from which I must ferret out the objects of my ambition, are not necessarily subjugated to my command or control or cajolery. Their thrust may be opposed to mine and their joy may lie in my being denied.

That is the source and support of fear in me. If you can recollect the one we left behind in meditation, him of the closed eyes and quiet disposition, his was a silent mind that was intent on overcoming limitation not by satisfaction of desires but by seeing himself as free of all desires. His method was to shift the focus of self-perception from its centre in the person that he had taken himself to be (on your pattern and mine), to the centre of an indivisible totality of consciousness, a 'total mind' if we can suffer the expression. And in the total, where is limitation? For limitation can only be in the part. And without limitation there can be no fear.

But he was playing a different ball-game called the silent mind. We are playing the game of an alert, awakened, poised mind, a power game of maximised potential. However, here too we need to be fearless. For fear disables us, deprives us of our strength when we most need it, and betrays the bastion from within.

In our game too we can, and shall, arrive at fearlessness. This we do by right understanding of the parts that make up the whole and their harmony in relationships. You and I need not step into the centre of totality to give meaning and direction to our chosen task (never forgetting the balance sheet). We need not attain limitlessness by positioning ourselves in (rather, as) a centre without a circumference. You and I can achieve our utilitarian purpose by accepting the truth of personal limitations, and by seeing its natural functioning in the scheme of things—in other words by SEEING WITH A CLEAR MIND THE LIMITS OF LIMITATION.

There is symphony in the orchestrated movement of ACTION which is a tidal wave flowing through Space for the entire duration of Time. It is the beginningless, endless causal flow of mentalised energy. In it fear has no place, no purpose, no sense. It is only the anxiety for gratification of personal desire, and the perceived possibility of its denial in the workings of totality, that generates fear. Let us face up to reality and just do our best within the limitations that man and mind are naturally subject to.

What is our objection to what is natural? What is there to fear in that?

21

face all problems equally

A graded value-scale is a creation of the mind. Those values that you bestow upon objects are not their inherent properties, but are superimpositions derived from your personal relationship with them. When dealing with those objects, which figure in the transactions of your life, you bring in likes and dislikes. Thus the activity which could and should be organised and manipulated in simple terms of factual evaluations, gets complicated by being transformed into mental moods of pleasure or resentment.

When your mind runs away from the task in front of you and engages itself in conjecture of probabilities and anxiety for results, there is blurring of perception and also a fear of failure. This fear generates anger that your wishes may not be fulfilled. Your energy is dissipated in this flood of thoughts and you feel uneven to the task, so you would like to escape responsibility for decision. You need to save face, and that is no problem, because the mind is good at offering you a variety of justifications. You say you need to recheck some facts, or that you need more details, or that it is evidently a situation where more time must be given for the elements to congeal. You decide you will get back to it next week.

You may as well wait for a cold candle to start burning by itself next week!

If your conclusions were honest, that would be a different thing. Then your calm and collected mind, focusing attention upon the single thought, would have given the answer, and you would have known in that stillness of a sharp intellect that to keep the matter pending was a positive and strong decision. But in the proposition we have narrated, we have posited a different scenario of an escapist which sadly is much more common.

If thus you have resorted to procrastination, how have you helped yourself? You will tend to occupy yourself with the easy, the pleasant, the totally controllable. These simpler matters would almost run their course anyhow, even without a decisive contribution from you. There will be many obvious, self-revealing problems in the daily routine of any organisation, and often the solutions for them flow naturally, provided a little effort is diverted towards them.

But there will be other problems that do not wear the trappings that proclaim their rank. They remain unnoticed, while ticking away menacingly in the complicated bowels of their workings. They even seem to have a perverse capability to hide themselves. He is truly a senior executive who can detect the minute manifestations of the presence of such problems before their hideous figures stand up for all to see with frightened eyes. He spots them in their hiding places amidst bushes or burrows, and grabbing them by the ear hauls them up into open view. He is not afraid to do so. He faces them stoically, for he has no fear. Even if they represent fearful possibilities, he deals with them to the best of his ability, for he knows and accepts that the world was not created to please and pamper him, that he should act promptly as well as he can, and the ultimate fruits are produced by a play of forces much vaster than any individual, and in having contributed his personal best, he has been a complete person.

Some desires will be fulfilled, some will be frustrated. The pleasant will come sometimes, the unpleasant at others. The unfolding action within the universal movement will never be a freak, but always the right resolution of all the energies that have shaped the action and contributed as causes to the ultimate shaping of the result. He who knows this performs without shackling himself in fetters of erroneous concepts that can only lead to mental agony of one's own creation.

the art of sleeping

It has been a long day, and it is time to relax. After a meal of sensible proportions and composition and some time spent pleasantly with the family—let us hope you listened more than you talked—it is time to sleep. It ought to be the simplest thing to do—to sleep. It is nature's lavish gift, enjoyed by all its creatures. The 'lowly' creatures do not ask for a drink, much less a sleeping pill. Nor, I honestly believe, do sheep count men.

What is sleep, deep sleep? It is the total cessation of thoughts. Your thought flow has to cease completely. As we have seen, thought is the first manifestation of the energy of consciousness, which is then translated into action. We are thinking machines. You are a fine-tuned high-powered eight cylinder machine. That is lovely in itself.

Now let us say you own (you probably do) a beautiful fine-tuned high-powered eight cylinder limousine. You use it all day to go to the office, to visit a work-spot, to run into the next town for a business contact. At the end of the day you drive the car into your garage. But suppose you do not switch off the motor, you leave it ticking and go to your room.

For all the pedigreed perfection of the machine, you are not being fair to it. Denied the freedom of movement upon the highway, now standing still, yet generating energy to no purpose, striving yet stagnating, the frustrated engine tends to get heated up. There is wear and tear in its futile exertion. And tomorrow, when you need all the efficiency of its known capability, the car may leave you stranded. Whose fault? Please look at yourself again carefully. In relationship to you, consciousness resides as your memory. It is the causal state. *IT IS BEFORE YOU ARE.* You are not where your memory is, you are where the remembrance is and that comes later. That is to say, memory puts forth its energy as a thought into which you (the individual that you are) are also structured as the subject that knows an object. This 'I-know' experience is the very sense of your personal 'I-am', the basis of your individualisation. All your concepts of the pleasant which you wish to perpetuate, and the unpleasant which you wish dead, are the essence of your memory, and their impress is upon the desires that rise up in you. Your memory fashions your desires from the sum total of its contents. Nothing is lost, nothing is added. What will surface when? The timing is a sequence of causal determinism, an infallible adherence to a law, just as the energies of electricity or magnetism or gravity eternally adhere to the laws of nature, which the science of physics has formulated for our understanding. Leave those depths and details, but let us understand this: consciousness is an energy, it implicitly follows its unvarying laws. As out of total electricity, there is a small part that flows into your house and serves your needs, there is a small chunk of conscious energy associated with you and that is your memory capability. When this is switched on, the light that glows is thought. In this light, objects become visible (the world is known) and transactions become possible. When it is switched off, there are no objects, there is no knowing. Therefore there is no knower. As you are structured into, and through, the process of knowing, at this point you, as the individuality, have ceased to manifest. That is the state of deep sleep. True, the physiological functions of breathing, circulation and digestion are maintained by a routine application of a small part of life energy, because sleep is a *pause,* not a *termination* of individuality which would be death. We intend to live another day and make another million, so why have I even brought up that scary word? Sorry.

If you lie in bed and helplessly the thoughts of business or relationships course through your head, you are parked in the garage but the engine is cranking. The tempo may conceivably go up to higher revolutions and in your intensity you may even be shifting into gear and releasing the clutch, while you are pressing down hard upon the brake pedal, in the sense that no movement into action is possible. The wheels cannot turn. What are you doing? If it is gentle rumination in your head, the engine is still running. Even if you have managed to doze off and have slipped into a dream state, know that dreams are thought processes no less than waking experiences, the flow continues. But in a dream (barring intense emotions or nightmares) the energy is of low wattage and the flow is a trickle (as electricity in a so-called zero watt night lamp). Granting at this stage that dreams are outside your control, we can overlook their notional disturbance. But we have to be concerned about the refusal of our waking mind to quieten down and cease altogether when we command it to do so. Why does the key jam in the ignition lock and prevent the switching off?

THE ART OF SLEEPING

The English language occasionally blunders into wise phrases! So rightly have the founders spoken of 'sound sleep', for, most of the time, our *sound* sleep is not the *silent* sleep that it is meant to be, but sleep filled with the sound of chattering thoughts that refuse to be stilled!

If we wish seriously to be efficient, to be energetic enough to achieve our ambitious targets, to remain fine-tuned for each tomorrow, then we should earn the blessing of sound sleep—read, silent sleep.

We can. By seeing clearly the rightness and beauty of life as it is, and thereby being able not merely to accept but indeed to love the cardinal truths of action and result. Let that love turn to a smile, let the smile turn to sleep ...

when the mind sleeps

Nature *is* total harmony. It is not through striving that nature developed such harmony. Rather it is the inherent total harmony that has been termed Nature.

There is hunger in Nature and there is food which eliminates hunger. There is thirst and also there is water which quenches thirst. There is the urge for perpetuation through offspring and there is the provision of union that permits reproduction. It is so because *all* of creation has emerged out of *one* source, one cause, one movement, one identity. All is well and nothing is amiss.

We are looking for harmony in the phenomenon in which there is mind and there is sleep.

Mind is motion, it is a cascade of constantly flowing thoughts. The prime mover setting up and sustaining this motion is desire. Desire is the method of your pursuit of happiness. Why do you want to pursue happiness? Ask that of yourself. Because it is your nature to be happy. You cannot rest till you are happy. But you are not happy as can be, because you have decided you need possessions, associations, relationships, to make you happy. Your conviction is that you are not self-contained and self-sufficient to abide in yourself in a state of undisturbed happiness, and therefore you seek such comfort through transactions with the world around you. That is the movement from within you into the environment, whose source is in memory, whose subtle manifestation is as thought (or idea) and which expresses itself at a gross level as action.

That is why you demand thought. You need it. It is the vehicle of your expression and your fulfilment. You have lived with this methodology of thought and action all your life and obviously, there is still a store house of desires. You find yourself subjected to an urge, or more rightly to a compulsion, to continue playing the game. (You tell yourself: 'Only till I hit the jackpot.' But we all know that the one who hits the jackpot is out there again cranking the lever or turning the wheel.) You do not know how to stop.

You (me too) are like a child that is so hooked on to a game that it will not come in from the garden though it is hungry and should take a respite. The mother has to cajole it, and even force it—for its own survival.

After a sufficient spell of striving which a full day is, even if the ultimate satisfaction has not been achieved (and it will never be), it is time that you cried a halt and retreated. Granted it is only to return later to the field, but at this moment the need is to still the movement, and allow the whole equipment, the body which is the vehicle through which the energy operates, to regain its cool equilibrium and mechanical efficiency. Stilling the movement cannot mean mere cessation of bodily activity which is a secondary effect, it must mean the cessation of thought at the primary level.

If that could be achieved by effort, which means if it were an act you could perform, then the action must be preceded by the thought of such action. So obviously thought cannot be ended by thought which can only perpetuate itself. This was anticipated in the harmony of Nature which built sleep into its processes.

So sleep is ready to reach out to you, and hold you in its folds secure from yourself and the agony of compulsive entanglement in the meshes of your thoughts even after you can no longer sustain the effort. Without sleep you would be like a runner condemned to keep running even after the marathon course has been covered and your knees are buckling and your lungs are bursting. 'Mother Nature' they say—you may be inclined to agree in this context, for the compassion is evident.

What then is your role and what makes even sleep a problem? It is your peevish petulant preoccupation with your desires long past the stage of utility. You should have the sense of distinguishing between the possible and the pointless. You must turn away from thoughts that are irrelevant to this moment, no matter how important they may be at another point of time. That is economy of thought. That is really conservation of energy. That is the prerequisite for efficiency. You should relax into the joy of just being. That relaxation has to be your contribution and Nature's bounty gives you the gift of sleep. You have to blame yourself if you wilfully persist with attention to your pursuits of happiness beyond the point where the pursuit itself has turned to agony.

That is simply stated. But how to effect this disinvestment now? Not by pleading with your pillow! For tonight, follow your own method. You can eliminate the light in your room by switching off the flow of current (the right way), or by breaking the bulb (the wrong way). Sleep possessing the stilled mind would be the right harmony that bestows happiness with strength. The alternative is to work on the body directly, (because you lack the courage and stamina to work on the mind,) and dull the ability of the equipment to manifest energy as action, and thus retard action till it comes to a halt. It is like throwing a spanner into the works to stop the turning wheels. And tomorrow the poor machine may run again, but on damaged sprockets. This is what we do to ourselves when we take easy recourse to the bottle or the pill, or else to diversions that take their toll of energy from our depleted reserves, but conceal the damage from immediate recognition because the change and the novelty give us an artificial boost.

Tonight, and for a few nights to come (with progressively diminishing dependence) manage as well as you can, but stay with the new-found awareness of the workings of the mind. All of us are creatures of habit, not because there is an inevitability in any pattern, but because we do not pause for analysis and re-evaluation.

My early cigarettes were quite pleasurable, so I looked forward to a smoke. Soon it became a habit, and not being able to smoke when I felt like it (twenty times a day) became a cause for distress. Till that day came (as it had to come), when the family doctor assessed my frame racked by bouts of boisterous cough, and said my lungs were coated thicker with tar than the driveway to my house and sweetly advised me to get on with my death wish because if I continued smoking (and why should I give up what I so relished?) my days were severely numbered.

Certainly my love for cigarettes did not turn to apathy that moment, but my *greater love* for life asserted itself. If only one of the twain could be had, for me it was life. So the habit died. (Shall I say, it perished without smoke.) The habit died and I lived.

Thus it is with our minds in all aspects. Left to itself the mind moves along the habituated lines, but alerted, it is transformed. There is a room full of dense darkness.

How much time is necessary to disperse all that load of darkness? The instant a light is lit, all the darkness vanishes. As light dispels darkness instantly, so does knowledge dispel ignorance. *It is not a function of time.* It is not the end product of prolonged activity. It is simultaneous with right understanding. That is why wise ancients have proclaimed that controlling the mind can be as easy as penetrating a flower petal with a sharp needle, and *at the same time* as difficult as lifting a mountain with one's hands! You always believed two-in-one is a bargain. You can keep this.

Convince yourself about the validity, strength and support of new factors that are made available to your understanding. Once convinced, stay deliberately with them. At first there will be only verbal appreciation, a periodic recollection. That state of *knowing* will get transformed into a state of *becoming,* when the knowledge would have *merged* into you and will operate spontaneously, without the intermediacy of memory or verbal construct. Then the old habit would be seen to have perished somewhere along the path, its grave unmarked.

We have focused on the need to sleep well and wake up refreshed, but actually the idea has only summed up the whole theme that we have been discussing all along. That was, how to live and work in the *PRESENT* to the exclusion of distracting and debilitating forays of the mind into recollections of the past and anxious anticipations of the future; how to interpose the *PAUSE* between action and reaction; how to accept the fruits of action as the right dispensation of the multiple workings of a unitary movement in which each individual is but a part. Thus we have formulated a clearly defined basis for the method of our mental operation. We have to live it now with conviction. It cannot be an interlude, it is the only way we shall live.

Such a mind would have mastered the art of switching off. Short periods of total stillness within the mind are more productive of renewed energy than long spells of listless sleep. Even during the waking hours of work, those pauses when the mind is stilled are really moments of contact with the power of consciousness. Tiresomeness is the result of wasteful anxiety and agitation, not of the productive activity.

This play of *'sleep'* interposed throughout the well-organised application of the mind to its work, this ability to withdraw into an inner stillness whenever the mind had no function to perform outside, releases unsuspected reserves of energy, enhances clarity of perception and felicity of performance, and makes light the tasks that seemed awesome before.

In the harmony of creation, mind was structured to serve the needs of the one that possessed it. Where will it go? What else will it do? But you too must understand that harmony and remain a part of it. Your mind will serve you in the rightful transformation of your past into your future in the continuity of the person that you are in the present. It is your imagination running contrary to the natural sequence that sets up a turbulence. Nature sees to it that, if you do not demand from your mind what you do not need, you will be provided, even without your asking, what you need.

24

leadership

One is a leader when there are followers. Authority may give you subordinates and servants, it may assemble a long line of bodies behind your body, but that is not the truth of leadership. The truth must be seen in the harmony of acceptance. A leader does not create a following; a following creates a leader. The man of destiny does not proclaim *'Accept me. Go with me. I am a leader.'* Clear in his own mind about the rightness of his goals and of his actions, dedicated to the attainment of clearly perceived objectives, he marches on. Somewhere along the journey he happens to look over his shoulder, more perhaps to confirm his loneliness, when to his amazement he finds many behind him. To his humble unspoken question, they speak up with one voice and say *'We trust you. We are with you on the path for the goal. You lead us. Let us march together.'*

This situation cannot be brought about by clever manipulation or planned strategy. Authority may bring you obedience, but it is your personality that harnesses many individuals into one coherent team and sustains their zeal to share your destiny. The lamp in the room fills the space with light, the flowers in the garden fill the air with fragrance. The lamp and the flowers do nothing but remain as themselves, yet their impact is felt upon the surroundings. So does the man of values, of truth, of honesty, by the mere fact of being himself, permeate the circle in which he exists, enhancing the worth of everything therein and uniting all.

Know yourself and be yourself. Only events can confirm to you the reality that is you. As one needs a mirror to see one's face, one needs the world to see the person that oneself is. Do not ever blame the mirror for what it reveals, it does not lie.

There can never be a failing of the followers, there can only be a failing of the leader. The leader fails when he acts without conviction. One should march to one's goal with such conviction of its rightness and such earnestness of desire for it, that there is total identity between the person and the objective. That is the name of love. Love may be regarded a feeble, or even a debilitating word in the vocabulary of hardheaded management, but that is so only when the soft-headed professor concludes that love is a contrived relationship. Shall we put aside for a moment the love in our hearts, and look instead at the heart of love? Then we will see that love is the very being of oneself. We love the things of the world because we love ourselves, and we want to eliminate sorrow to the self we love in us, when this 'myself' is unhappy lacking something that the world has and will be happy once that is possessed. We strive to acquire it, so that the loved myself is satisfied and at peace. All of living is only this pursuit. 'I love you' has always meant that you are the cause of making me feel good and complete within myself (where I exist) and this feeling in myself is what I want for my own sake, and so I love you as the means of loving myself. It is never different.

You may ask: If it is never different, why then do you belabour the obvious and tell me this now?

We have to focus attention on it, because, though love of self is unchanging, we deceive ourselves about what is the input we are really demanding to please the self. Thus we really want leisure but pretend security but proclaim we are willing to venture forth whether we succeed or fail. We remain rigid but declare that others should be flexible—be reasonable, we tell them. The results are naturally the arithmetic of the positive and the negative factors all put together, and of course, in this sequence, the left hand has undone much of what the right hand has done.

When there is clarity of perception and earnestness of purpose, you are integrated. Therefore, there is joy and fulfilment in the doing itself, which enables seeing the result as a *fact* and not as a *failure*. Such a mind retains its mastery over itself, and therefore, remains the undaunted master of the unfolding situation.

The relationship that is spontaneously nurtured between such a mind and the minds of those around who wish to share the aspirations, and find strength and direction therein, is the manifestation of love in activity or in togetherness. Here the love of self of all the participants is served by the common work ethic and since each is happy in himself, all are happy together. We have an acknowledged leader and an efficient team.

So, how do you make yourself a great leader? *YOU DON'T*. Instead, just be yourself. To deal with things, you need knowledge. To deal with people, you need sympathy. But to deal with yourself, you need nothing; just be yourself. And the amazing truth will then manifest, that thereby you gain access to the knowledge and the sympathy you need in the rightful process of your becoming. Consequently, if others make you their leader, you will hear about it. Do not go asking for it.

Once when a wounded bird had taken refuge in the protective hands of the Buddha, an offensive Devadatta came to him claiming it for himself. Lord Buddha said, *'The bird is mine ... the first of myriad things which shall be mine by right of mercy and love's lordliness'*—a prophecy whose fulfilment the world has witnessed. Mark the words 'love's lordliness'. We need to find a place for it in our balance sheet.

harmony amidst change

We tend to allot pride of place to consistency in a person. A good quality no doubt, if rightly understood. Surely it cannot mean that one remains pegged to one idea, one judgement, one hypothesis all one's life and makes a virtue of it. In a world of relationships where the others are constantly changing in attitudes and affections and affiliations, and in a world of knowledge where perceptions and techniques are varying, while you yourself at the centre of this flux are an entity with desires and demands that blow like a shifting breeze, what can consistency mean?

It cannot be a stillness. Nor can it be a disorganised turmoil of irreconcilable forces forever tugging in opposite directions. It has to be a dynamic balance, wherein each movement is represented while the whole is accepted by all the parts.

If you are standing on the roadside and a friend is suddenly sighted peddling past you upon a bicycle, and you shout at him *'Hey, I have something important to tell you'* by then he is already too far away to have heard and heeded your intent. But if you were riding a bicycle in the same direction when he unnoticingly went past you, and you purposefully spurted and caught up with him, and the two of you moved alongside at the same speed (minding the traffic), you could converse with all the felicity of a sojourn on a park bench and even place a patronising arm upon each other's shoulders. In the relative motion there could be consistency of purpose and performance. In the same way the orbiting satellite is manoeuvred into geostatic position with the restless earth as both sweep through space, and in the camaraderie thus established there is scope for the most courteous communication for the benefit of mankind.

Getting back upon our bicycles, if you happen to be in a mood to pedal away furiously and your more rotund friend is already panting, if your need to communicate is genuine, there is no other way but for you to slow down. Coaxing or demanding an acceleration that is not possible can only precipitate an angry scene or a heart ailment. Adjustment is the name of peace, and adamancy the name of grief.

The flooded river is flowing with visible velocity. You are standing upon the bank and watching. A piece of driftwood comes floating along. It offers no resistance to the current and is carried in the waters, shifting with them, swirling with them, one with their movement. It goes where the river goes.

But you are standing there with a set purpose. You have important work to do at a spot that is fifty yards upstream from where you are standing, on the OTHER SIDE of the river. From your home you could reach the bank only at this point as the rest of the terrain was inaccessible. Normally you could wade across the shallow flow. Today there were flash floods and you had not provided for this situation. Now the urgent task must be completed.

You are a fairly good swimmer. True.

The current is rather strong. Equally true.

What do you do? Being the reasonable man that you are, you enter the waters, and calmly though firmly you stroke your way across. You certainly do not draw a straight line to the upstream point you wish to reach (though you know that the straight line is the shortest distance between two points, and you are a no-nonsense man) and thrash your hands and legs for all you are worth in a frenzied determination to do or die. You do not even set your sights on a point directly opposite to where you are standing. Instead you navigate along a diagonal that may land you fifty feet downstream. You actually befriend and utilise the energy of the flood by harmonising your own energy with it so that your purpose may be served through optimum efficiency in a spirit of cooperation. While the river tends to carry you downstream (as it carried the unprotesting dead wood), you steer yourself along its width through deft strokes of your arms. And in due course you reach the other bank. Scrambling up and smiling, even pleasantly exhilarated, you now walk along on the other side of the river to your chosen destination. It is now a hundred feet away but on plain ground and that is no problem.

It would have been vanity (always a form of suicide) to have proclaimed *'I never go back—not me'* and defied the might of the flood to traverse the straight line. It would have been disastrous folly to have grossly overestimated one's own muscle or underestimated the seething strength of opposing forces. It would have been self-defeating inertia to have lightly concluded that overwhelming odds had deprived you of your rightful goals and returned home. Cowardice is not prudence.

In every situation there is a right balance. Attaining that is fulfilment. In the beginningless and endless flow of action which is the unbroken movement of the energy of life, fulfilment is not described by the fruit, it is described by the harmony. And that is not the insipid surrender of an insentient log to whatever force impels its drift; it is the matching of your will to reality to manifest in action the dynamic equation of *heroic harmony*.

why? because...

You cannot take it. Of all things, why did *this* have to happen? Why to *me*? Why just *now*?

Why did that fellow have to lie to me, me of all people, when I trusted him? You are disgusted ...

Why did the taxi-cab have to break down now when I am already behind time to catch my flight for the one meeting I just can't afford to miss? You are agitated.

Why did I have to slip and sprain my ankle so badly when I was looking forward eagerly to the delightful party? You pity yourself.

Why did I not confirm the order for that machine which was as good as new and going cheap, and pay an advance? I hesitated and now it is gone. Why did I miss the chance? You are full of regret.

Why did she have to tell her folks they were welcome to come and stay with us any time that suited them? I am stuck with them now for a week and it certainly does not suit me. You are angry as can be. (And most of us who have in-laws will sympathise.)

WHY in this sense is not an admissible question. It is in truth a mood rather than a query. It is not an enquiry into the constituent facts of the occurrence, it is an objection to the occurrence itself, denying its validity. It is your assertion that what happened had no business to happen.

You are not investigating the *causes* that led to the occurrence, which is not a futile pursuit if the answers can enhance your understanding or guide your further action. In saying why, oh why, in the manner of your saying it, you are questioning CAUSATION, which is the ordained methodology of all causing everywhere and at all times.

The answer to any 'why' begins with 'because', does it not? Thus all questions have a common answer. 'Because' is *'be-cause'* meaning 'cause being so'. The answer always is: such being the cause is the reason why this has happened.

The movement of life, which means of all occurrences, is from cause to effect. This is the direction of the flow of energy. To know that it is so is the basis of harmony with the law of nature. To march with it is progress. But to stand within the effect and to keep looking back furtively over the shoulder of Time at the past where the cause resided before it manifested as the present effect, is an exercise in futility. It is then not a rational determination by you of connected causes for constructive action, but 'causation-hunting'. It is an endless regression that ultimately phrases itself into asking *'why should causation be?'* or *'why was causation caused?'* The answer, if one is offered, can only be as right as the question is right in its conception. And in any case it does not help us in our pursuit of profit. What is of practical relevance to us is the clear understanding that defiance of the law of cause–effect continuum, or frustration over it, deprives us of the energy we should retain to deal with unfolding occurrences, however unexpected they may be. Indeed, it is exactly then and there that the maximum efficiency that one is capable of should be commandeered into service, and you choose such a moment to deprive yourself and defeat yourself. And then go on to accuse fate or bad luck or the devil of having conspired against a gullible innocent.

'Causation-hunting' is regression in time and so can go on as far back as time stretches into the past. The end of eternity is not reachable and if reached would not be of use to our purposes which need time for their fulfilment. It is enough to know that time is the medium of the mind for its progress upon its chosen path of quenching its desire through action. The awareness of desire, the planning and performance of action, the materialising of the fruits of action, and participation in the result—all this is the unchanging sequence of cascading effects of precedent causes. To move forward upon the current, meeting it and matching it, is the secret of right action from the individual's standpoint; not moving backwards into causal origins.

You come home from work, later today, than you are generally late anyhow, and none too pleased. Your seven-year-old son meets you at the door.

Why so late today dad?

I had to wait and get through with an important international call, my son.

Why did you have to wait dad?

I had to finalise a contract son.

Why did you have to ... have to ... contract?

You won't understand all that, my boy.

Why won't I understand all that dad?

(Enough is enough, you feel, still composed.)

That is enough, son.

Why is that enough, dad?

Because, you say, because...(you are looking for something to throw at him ...) because.

You have wisely answered the whole sequence of questions, and for all times, and for all humanity. Stop it there and glory in the discovery. The ultimate answer has shaped itself, out of your own mouth!

Be-cause. *Full-stop.* Cause creates its own rightful effect.

Why not deal the same way with all situations in life and *live* this wisdom instead of only lisping it? Is it all right for you to turn yourself into a seven-year-old upon the stage of life, asking why so? why so?

Instead, face the fact. Roll up the sleeves, feature half a smile, and calmly assess your response to the unfolding scenario. If you are in full control of yourself you have access to the maximum control of the situation that is available to you within the revealed parameters. Of course one does not decently ask for the impossible, one seeks to obtain the best that is available. And that best is available to the poised mind, not to the mind that is beating the forehead in despair or anger. Deal with the situation as it is, a fact confronting you, a fruit that is true to the tree on which it grew, a reality in the rightness of connected causes. Nothing is wrong with it, except your wrong wish that it should be otherwise. One needs to be man enough to accept that, even to be ashamed to resent it.

Action, obviously, is in the present. If you are dwelling in the past, or dreaming of the future, that still signifies your mental action in the present. There is no way you can be in the past or in the future, you are inevitably in the present. Thus depending upon how you utilised all the present moments that now stand linked in your memory as your past, you have been the architect of your life. Out of this totality is crystallising the reality of this very moment, the imminent experience. *HOW YOU DEAL WITH THIS PRESENT* moment will shape your future. You have a certain freedom of will, a certain span of choice, without violating the continuing identity of the person and personality that you are. There is no time to be reviewing, much less disputing, the limitations that are inherent, when the call is for decision and action within the ample freedoms that are vouchsafed to you.

If there is a 'fate' that they tell you cannot or will not deviate, then you tell them *fate is fated* to run its course, not me. Poor fate! But how does that bother us? Don't you feel *within yourself* your freedom and your choices and your energy for action?

Trust it and act on. Only do not be your own foe through despair and despondency. You are answerable for your future, having been the architect of your past. The present is the moment of truth.

one last word
(about lost words)

We are coming to the end of our stroll together during which we have talked of many things. Explicitly we have taken an analytical look at several aspects of our living and functioning that we had taken for granted hitherto. The unknown is brought into our knowing by diligent application of what is already known. One does not ask for proofs of the unknown—what validity would the answers have to the questioner?—rather, one settles down to re-examine what one had accepted as proofs of what one knew already. The clarity that grows thereby contains the promptings of 'new' knowledge. We have done this with ourselves.

In the process we have attempted to understand how and why we are, each one of us, the particular individual that one is, the energy-system of manifesting consciousness, the memory-bundle with specific desires and demands, the planning and executing intelligence, the participant in action, the responding emotional entity of joy and sorrow, of anger or affection, of greed or generosity. All that about 'ME' was vital information before we could chart our future to secure our goal of an improved balance sheet.

With this enhanced perception of 'person' and 'personality' we could discard the blinkers of habit and gaze with fresh wonder and delight at the realities of our life, which revealed to us one unitary movement of cause – effect flow in place of our earlier unthinking acceptance of isolated spheres of unrelated activity. And in that movement was the working of one giant machine in which a thousand wheels meshed and turned in tuned harmony.

Being able to see that took the strain off us, which had been imposed unproductively by the mistaken notion of false power centres, and the relaxation gained by right understanding resulted not only in an easy movement of frictionless flow, but also in the joyous hum of synchronised mechanics that represented maximum efficiency. In the process, *doership* was assigned its exact place, not an unbridled individuality that could desire anything it wished to, demand anything, and imagine that WILL could turn all wheels to its dictates. Such a mistaken notion of management only created turbulence and set up eddies in the smooth flow of related responses, causing and inviting resistance and resentment, thereby defeating itself.

Like chicks that emerge when their time has come by breaking the shell *from within,* we cracked the confines in which our WORDS were held captive by habituated usage and enabled their emergence into a world of sunlit freedom where the limbs could be stretched.

Then *ego* became a partner in an immensity, not an isolated defender amongst a horde of enemies. *Action* became a harmonious blending in a ceaseless flow, not an arbitrary self-serving. *Dynamism* became a spreading wave moving out from a steady kinetic centre, not the frantic fury of turbulent motion sweeping away its centre with itself. *Progress* gained its intuition and its instruction from the *pause* that altered reaction to reasoned action.

Meditation became the hub whose relative immobility supported the whirling rim of the wheel of action, not a passive state distanced from all connotations of activity. *Problems* became misnomers for situations that were eminently the right culmination of precedent causes, not confirmed errors compounded by the workings of cosmic caprice. The prime import of *economy* became the limited expenditure of the energy of consciousness as the outflow of thought just sufficient for the purpose on hand, not merely the conservation of the physical performance of work, or of the financial outlay of money and manpower. The concept of the *absolute* became subordinate to the compulsions of relativity in the inescapable structuring of the mind; not the other way round, that the mind could comprehend, and somehow accommodate that which could be termed truly and absolutely *ABSOLUTE*. *Leadership* became the gift of trust and acceptance from the enchanted following, not that the following was a creation and creature of the leader. The question *why* provided its own only answer, ending for evermore a futile distraction and thereby diverting attention to purposeful response. And trust in oneself became the true significance of *faith* that propels mentation into firm action.

Thus mental beliefs and behavioural norms that seemed to be the only positive and productive indices turned suspect, or even withered under scrutiny into negative and pretentious agents. Perceptions which had hitherto been condemned as negative by clothing them with word symbols that represented the negative side of our relative values, suddenly came alive as the positive possessors of strength and beauty and utility. The mind of man once shaped words to serve its purposes, but rigid words prove hostile and trick the unwary mind into errors. That is the tragedy of easy accedence to habit, which is the thoughtless surrender of the king to the slave, of sentient intelligence to insentient Time.

Let it not be said that you have figuratively 'killed time', musing idly over polemics.

Let it be said to your credit that in a truer act of introspective heroism you have *really* killed Time.

If only you were willing to listen, I could have told you how Time is a myth that aspires to eternity by fooling the credible victim to believe that he has been subjugated by Time, whereas in truth Time is but the present instant *existing in and through his conscious thought and dependent on his presence.* But now you are not in the mood for it. My dearest wish is that you may want to know ... at some other time! I hope we meet again.

28

epilogue

One last question is lingering upon your lips, and it is not difficult to guess what it is. You are wondering how all this fits your specific question. The whole response has been to introduce you to yourself, to explain to you the higher potential that lies in you, and to convince you that your access to it was never blocked. The change that an enlightened appreciation of the truth of yourself could bring about, has been held aloft as the one requirement to enhance your performance and improve your balance sheet. It is *your* contribution that has been coaxed all along.

Where is GOD in all this?—for your question, you will have me remember, was: *'Can God improve my balance sheet?'*

My friend, the focus of my reply throughout has stayed consistently on G-O-D, but at no stage could I venture to reveal that to you openly, for the word was suspect in your hardened misunderstanding and you would have accused me of being a bigoted peddler of religion, trying to trick you through false credentials and attempting to smuggle in *my* perverse God into *your* house through the back door. You will give me credit for having diligently avoided the proscribed word, till you have yourself now referred to it. And now I have your permission, I take it to tell you that the word *GOD* stands for the Reality, the ultimate Truth, the Absolute, Fact (beyond falsified imagination), the True Nature of oneself, the Source, Sustenance and Significance of life that is even now experienced by you. And by me. By all. That is what God stands for in all religions of all ages in all climes, revealed to us repeatedly (though infrequently) by those who used their wisdom to abide in the source of their consciousness without being carried away in its outpourings, and thereby came to experience the other dimension, the other plane of awareness, which we are denying to ourselves for want of interest, or more correctly, due to interest only in the material balance sheet. Them we call the Sages. But then the choice is ours and available. Who is to fault us for taking our pick? And why should they fault us?

I am only saying that the line of thinking that stretches from *PERSON* to *GOD* naturally passes through progressive levels of performance towards perfection, and so every step taken along the path bestows its blessing. To proceed upon the journey into the unfamiliar terrain, one should know and willingly obey the laws of the land, which is why we have looked meticulously at the energy that functions *through* the mind and *as* the mind. If you are busy otherwise, God (or gods) can wait. God has all the Time! For He owns Time. You are owned by Time.

Go, wander. Enjoy the landscape. Have a nice journey!